THE
PERFECT
LETTER

Scott, Foresman Business Writing Series

THE
PERFECT
LETTER

Patricia H. Westheimer
Robert B. Nelson

SCOTT, FORESMAN AND COMPANY
Glenview, Illinois   London

Library of Congress Cataloging-in-Publication Data

Westheimer, Patricia H.
  The perfect letter / Patricia H. Westheimer, Robert B. Nelson.
    p.   cm.
  ISBN 0-673-38879-4
  1. Commercial Correspondence.   2. Business writing.   I. Nelson,
Robert B.   II. Title.
HF5721.W465   1990
651.7′5 – dc20   89–10255
1 2 3 4 5 6 KPF 94 93 92 91 90 89   CIP

ISBN 0-673-38879-4

Scott, Foresman professional books are available for bulk sales at quantity discounts.
For information, please contact the Marketing Manager, Professional Books Group,
Scott, Foresman and Company, 1900 East Lake Avenue, Glenview, IL 60025.

FOREWORD

Whether you are one of thousands of employees or are working on your own, written communication can be crucial to the success of your company. At the very least, poorly written correspondence wastes time and reduces efficiency through misunderstandings and unnecessary follow-up phone calls and letters. Poor communication can also result in costly confrontations with customers and other key audiences, and can even doom a great new idea or product.

In contrast, clear, concise, and accurate writing is both efficient and cost effective. When people know precisely what you mean to say, you foster good will, better customer relations, and improved efficiency.

Good written communication does not come easy. But with this book by Pat Westheimer and Bob Nelson, you will find virtually all the help you need in writing exactly what you mean to say—precisely, accurately, and with just the right tone. It is written in a warm, friendly manner as it takes you through the various stages of planning, writing, and refining external correspondence.

An important key to your success in learning and improving is the authors' simple three-step approach to writing: Plan It, Write It, and Refine It. It is a totally natural way to write—similar to the way you speak. A second key is the quick outlines for many types of letters to assist you in formulating just the right message for a given set of circumstances. Still another key is the many excellent examples of letters that demonstrate the wrong and right ways of solving written communication problems.

As you read this book and learn new techniques for writing, begin to use them in your day-to-day correspondence. Use only what's comfortable at first. But as you become more proficient, be daring and try other techniques. Before long, you will be writing like a professional—leaving problems such as ambiguities and misinterpretations far behind.

There is a great need for clear, efficient communication in business today. The challenge is now yours to make it happen.

James W. Jacoby
President, Management
Communications Consultants
Bloomington, Minnesota

PREFACE

Writing is one of the most challenging and rewarding skills you can ever learn as a professional. You can learn to be an effective writer if you have the desire, but more importantly, the patience, to apply relatively few guidelines and rules with consistency.

The guidelines: plan, write, and refine.

The rules: write the way you speak, get to the point, be clear and concise, and be positive.

This book — and all effective writing — is built on these rather simple principles. They are easy to learn but difficult to apply on an ongoing basis.

You can learn much more from this book as well — techniques and tricks that can make your writing easier, examples to pattern your letters after, exercises to fine-tune writing skills — but none of these points are as important as the rules we've just stated.

Many people feel that writing is a dry, boring activity. Nothing could be further from the truth! Writing is a powerful communication skill that once mastered will help you to be more effective in all aspects of your life. Learning to write better can help you to realize your potential in life — for life!

We have several decades of writing experience between us, including some 20 books, and numerous magazine and newspaper articles, business plans, promotional pieces, and thousands upon thousands of business letters. We teach business writing in corporate and academic settings to students who write for many purposes, including research papers, informational and analytical reports, memorandums, proposals, business plans, and correspondence.

This book pulls together the best we have to offer on the topic of writing business letters. It is arranged in a chronological order that parallels the writing process. Reference materials and writing exercises are included at the end of each section, as well as numerous sample letters throughout, and a style guide that covers a wide range of grammar and punctuation rules in the appendices.

We hope this book will help you to more easily write effective business letters, and serve as an ongoing reference for the rest of your writing career. Once you master the skill of writing, you'll find it to be a skill you can be proud of, a skill that can help you achieve your personal and professional goals, and a skill you can also have fun with. Writing has been this and more for both of us, and we are only too happy to share what we've learned with you.

Patricia H. Westheimer
Robert B. Nelson

ACKNOWLEDGMENTS

Thank you for your support both professionally and personally: Jennifer Wallick, Julius and Dorrit Westheimer, Gloria Westheimer, Sara Baldwin, Dorothy Allen, Juliette Chandler, Anne Goshen, Jim Mastro, and Amy Davis.

The authors especially thank James W. Jacoby, President of Management Communications Consultants in Bloomington, Minnesota for his assistance in the development of materials for use in this book.

We have also learned many things from the thousands of students we have collectively taught in companies and on college campuses. Many of their letters are included in this book, both as a tribute to the students and because they were excellent letters!

Special thanks also to Al McCormick who assisted greatly in the preparation of this book.

CONTENTS

INTRODUCTION

In a nationwide survey conducted by a communications consulting firm, 79 percent of responding business executives listed the ability to write as the single most neglected skill in business; 53 percent rated their own writing ability as poor; and 59 percent rated the correspondence they received as poor or fair.

Why is business writing such a problem?

The answer may be different for each businessperson, but in general, the answer is some combination of a lack of knowledge or experience about effective writing principles, and a lack of confidence in applying those principles. Sixty percent of the respondents of this survey spent an average of nine or more hours per work week on business correspondence. That would be fine, even commendable, if time spent meant results. But customarily it doesn't. Managers, administrators, and secretaries complain that much of their writing time involves agonizing and redoing rather than creating and refining. Even worse, most claim that when they are finished, they are not satisfied with what they have written.

Every day business people face the dilemma of having to write effective letters. They have to write, but they don't know how. They put words down, knowing they aren't the right ones, hoping no one will notice. But people *do* notice. Millions of dollars and thousands of hours are lost each week on words that never communicate exactly what needs to be said. Sentences are so lengthy and awkward that readers rarely have time to sift through them for the crucial message. Ambiguities cause misinterpretations of straightforward information.

Now think about the next letter you have to write. Are you looking forward to composing it? Probably not. Most people dread writing projects because they:

○ Don't know how to begin

○ Struggle to find the right words to use

○ Try to write perfectly from the start

○ Wrestle with proper punctuation and spelling

Writing doesn't have to be difficult. It doesn't have to take the enormous energy and frustration that most people expend for bland, mediocre results. There is another way. This book shows you how to streamline the writing process to produce effective letters with minimal effort.

When was the last time you received a well-written letter? Or wrote one? With this book, you can do both. *The Perfect Letter* describes the following three-step recipe for writing:

1. Plan It.

2. Write It.

3. Refine It.

Then you're finished. These three steps give you an action plan for letters and other writing projects, including memos, reports, lengthy proposals — almost anything you have to write.

The exciting thing about this approach is that it teaches you to write the way you always wanted to but believed you couldn't, or were told you shouldn't. Most business writers think they must use pompous, wordy language to sound important and get their messages taken seriously. They strive to *impress* rather than *express*. Actually, the opposite is true. The best business writing is *simple* and *clear*—and don't let anyone ever tell you otherwise!

Consider the difference between the following letter excerpts:

> *Poor:* It is realized that you will have to effect numerous modifications to current procedures expeditiously.

> *Better:* You will have to change current procedures at once.

Which letter would you want to receive? Why? The first might work fine for a Ph.D. dissertation on management, but the second gets the point across much more clearly and simply—and thus with greater power.

The Perfect Letter offers a practical plan to banish your writing troubles. Follow this three-part process, and you're on your way to being the writer you've always admired. Many very fine business writers admit they don't have fancy techniques. They keep their writing simple. They write the way they speak using conversational words and simple sentences, and stop when they've said what they want. A group of successful corporate presidents agreed that the three most important aspects of their writing include brevity, clarity, and *personal warmth*.

Our three-part plan produces the results you want. What's the method? Plan It, Write It, Refine It. How long does it take? Only as long as it takes you to read this book! You'll see how to remove all the stuffy words and complex phrases from your writing and shift from pompous to powerful, from meaningless to meaningful.

Who can use these tips? Anyone who communicates on paper! That spans everyone from corporate executives to clerical assistants to ghostwriters. When asked, most people claim that writing feels painful, takes too much time, and rarely yields results. That's because most writers start with no real plan, and write words suitable for government manuals, but not for a 60-second letter. Such writers lose their audience before they begin. No wonder their writing seems so awkward. Now, you have the opportunity to learn an easier way. And as you'll soon see, it's so easy!

Many self-proclaimed "good writers" are those who turn out lengthy letters filled with "businessese" that no one wants to wade through or try to understand. Oftentimes, less confident people show up for writing seminars able to produce the same message as their more pretentious colleagues, in half the space, with half the syllables, and no one misses their message. Why? Because they rely upon their ears as their guide to effective writing. They haven't been brainwashed, or business-washed, into thinking that they have to sound unusually educated or superior on paper. As a result, they communicate much more clearly, naturally, and correctly. Clear communication is essential in the business world.

Writing the great American novel could be an involved, inspired task, but writing clear, effective business letters is more a function of consistently applying a few principles of effective writing. Learn these principles, and transform your writing today.

In this book we're going to give you the same tools we give to our clients and students in business writing seminars. All the examples come from actual companies. The names have been changed, but the problems are universal. The tips presented in this book work for them, and they'll work for you. When you write using our plan, everything from the shortest letter to the most complex report shows the signs of an accomplished, confident writer—you!

PART ONE

Plan It

CHAPTER 1

Think

WHAT'S YOUR PURPOSE?

WHO'S YOUR AUDIENCE?

WHAT DO YOU WANT TO ACHIEVE?

So you have to write a letter. It's up to you to communicate clearly, concisely, correctly. But how?

Initially you need to clarify just what a letter is—and isn't. The worst of all writing experiences occurs when business professionals spend hours composing, only to find that they have missed the main point, haven't targeted their audience, or haven't used the proper format. Remember, you're writing a letter—not a memo, meeting minutes, or a report.

One of the biggest mistakes you can make is to assume that you are going to turn out perfect copy without any prior thought or planning. It is a great fallacy to believe that good writing should flow with the ease of ink from your pen! It is closer to the truth to compare good writing with the activity of farming. Every farmer knows that to yield an effective crop there must be preparation, planting, and harvest. For a farmer to skip any of these steps would seem ridiculous.

Likewise, effective writing requires initial preparation. The first part of this preparation involves *thinking*. The basis of clear writing is clear thinking.

Before you begin to write a business letter, ask yourself and think about these three basic questions:

○ What's my purpose?

○ Who's my audience?

○ What action do I want?

Purpose is the *reason* for writing. Whether you're writing to inform or inquire you need to stay on target and not lose focus.

Your audience *receives* your message. In most business letters, this is usually a single individual.

The desired action helps determine exactly what you want to have happen as a *result* of your letter. If you know and specifically ask for what you want, chances are increased that you'll get it!

WHAT'S YOUR PURPOSE?

It's important to have your purpose in mind before you begin to write. Once your purpose is clear, the organization and focus of your letter become easier to determine. Are you writing to inform, respond, refute, inquire, direct, or persuade? In some instances, after you consider your purpose, you might opt not to write a letter at all but instead to make a telephone call, schedule a personal visit, or drop the matter entirely!

One of the main pitfalls in letter writing is trying to do too much at one time. A letter that attempts to give information on a new topic, respond to a previously discussed problem, and suggest unrelated administrative changes both confuses the reader and weakens each topic.

The following letter tries to do too much:

May 3, 19XX

Ms. Jane Olson
Manager, Operations
ABC Company
1234 Oak Avenue
New York, NY 10072

Subject: HRD CONSULTING

Dear Ms. Olson:

We have been very busy lately, and I haven't been
able to get out several letters, so I decided to condense some major items into one letter.

Overtime—This category seems excessive for your
size and type of business. Let's discuss.

At next Monday's meeting we will discuss new
benefit/options and their costs—more to follow on
this.

Profit-sharing—The profit-sharing allocations are
out. My assistant will send you your copy. This
program seems to be well received throughout the
organization.

Sincerely,

CJ Conley
Consultant

To solve this problem, write a separate letter on each
topic mentioned and more fully discuss each topic. Give
your letters a single focus and a single purpose. Imagine
that you are the recipient, not the writer!

WHO'S YOUR AUDIENCE?

The audience is one of the most important factors to
consider when planning your writing. It is also the one
area most people overlook.

What's the best way to bridge the gap between speaking and writing? You will never write very well if you don't tailor your communication to your recipients. One of the latest business writing trends is called "reader-based" writing. In other words, you write for your reader rather than for yourself. This is a critical orientation to remember at the beginning of any writing project.

One of the most common elements in business letters is the overuse of the pronoun "I": most letters begin with and are consumed with "I." Now, how important is "I" to the reader? Not very. Successful salespeople know to target their product or their service to their customers. This is the key to get them to buy and use the product. The same holds true for effective writers. Instead of using "I," "me," "us," or "we," why not focus instead on "you," "your," client's name, or client's concern? Look at the following letter excerpt and notice how consumed the writer is with the word "I." Then, refocus on "you" and notice the difference.

EXCESSIVE "I"

I was reviewing your department's travel deductions and I found too many unverified deductions. Please consult me concerning these errors.

A VARIETY OF PRONOUNS

When you travel on business, keep a log of your business expenses. We can reimburse you faster if there are fewer unverified vouchers. Thanks for your help!

Here's a quick tip. If it's too difficult to write in your audience's voice, do your first draft in your own. Then when you revise your letter, change your orientation from writer-centered to reader-centered.

There are three main questions to answer when considering your audience:

1. What does the reader already know about the topic?
2. What does the reader need to know to satisfy your purpose?
3. What is the reader's likely attitude toward the topic?

Answering these questions will only take a few moments of your time, and will be an excellent investment of your energy.

ALREADY KNOWN.   The first question to ask about your reader is how much he or she knows about the topic being discussed in the letter. When readers are familiar with your topic, you won't need to write in great detail. In these cases, concentrate on succinctness. Try this technique: Imagine there's a charge for each word you use, as though you're sending a telegram. Your brevity will improve your writing. We've read letters that began, "As you already know . . ." or, "To refresh your memory . . ." Leave these phrases out. They could insult the reader who probably remembers your topic quite clearly. Don't tell readers information they already know! This will cause them to "tune out" and possibly miss important, new information you are trying to relate. Any "questionable" background material can be included as an attachment to your clear, crisp, concise letter.

But what do you do about an audience that's not knowledgeable? Attempt to assess the exact extent of their familiarity with your material and fill in the empty areas accordingly. That's difficult, though, especially when the knowledge levels of multiple readers are diverse.

If you are writing letters to a diverse group, you can choose from a couple of alternatives: either subdivide the group, and devise several specific letters, one for each group; or compose a single comprehensive message aimed at the group's least knowledgeable members, that is, the group's "common denominator."

NEED TO KNOW. After you eliminate the information your readers already know, fill in what they *need to know* in order to respond effectively to your letter. This may include all the information needed for the reader to make a decision, take a certain action, or continue with his or her work. A letter that requires the reader to seek additional information or clarification in order to take the next action is poorly written—it defeats the purpose of writing the letter to begin with!

LIKELY ATTITUDES. A final question to ask about your readers is what is their likely attitude about you or the topic of your letter. How do they feel about your topic? Is their attitude positive, neutral, or negative?

If a reader is likely to disagree with your topic and proposed action, you will need to provide more persuasive arguments and data and perhaps more information than if the reader is already predisposed to your topic and/ or request.

Positive or negative, however, the important point is that ignoring the attitude of the audience can get you in trouble as a writer. Nothing is more discouraging than receiving a letter that's been written with no particular person in mind. It can cause your colleagues to feel ne- glected, discounted, and downright insulted! Win them over with a personalized, individualized approach, and they'll look forward to reading your letters!

OTHER CONSIDERATIONS. There are a number of secondary considerations you should make about your readers, including age, gender, education, and occupation. Knowing this information about your readers can help you to write a more informed letter that is tailored to the reader.

Age. If you use an example from the 1960s, you can count on not reaching a certain percentage of your recipients. If you employ a colloquial expression that you stole from your sweet 16-year-old daughter, don't be surprised when the adults on your distribution list won't take you seriously.

A manager at a major West Coast hotel generated the following excerpt from a letter. Some of his more sophisticated employees found it juvenile. (Needless to say, the grammar, punctuation, and spelling errors didn't help him either.)

> *Poor:* December is turning out to be a far out month for the hotel, both occupancy and rate-wise. One of the reasons this month will be so good is because of the BUSINESS ROUNDTABLE GROUP. Everyone associated with this group is listed in the FORTUNE 500, some of the most classy companies in the world.
>
> What we have here is a fantastic opportunity. With over 400 people paying to use our facilities they will also be checking out our property for some of their future business meetings. By doing what we do best, being friendly, efficient and professionals, the business we could generate in the years to come is endless.
>
> SO LET'S ALL PITCH IN AND DO THE BANG-UP JOB THAT WE ARE ALL CAPIBLE (sic) OF DOING!!!!!!!!!!!!!!!!!!!!!!!!!

Gender. Knowing the gender of your audience can make a difference in your tone and expressions. Business letters should avoid sexual stereotyping and treat everyone as professionals. Always read your letters as though you are the recipient. Do you feel left out or offended? If so, modify the letter to correct these problems.

Education. If you are writing to a well-educated audience, you don't necessarily need to use sophisticated, academic language. In fact, most every reader appreciates reading material that is clear, concise, and easy to understand.

When analyzing the readability levels of newspapers, for example, the actual wording is not at the education level that the readers possess. Why is this? Knowledgeable editors and writers know that in order for an audience to understand and quickly act on the information, the writing cannot be too lofty and abstract.

You will not appear undereducated when you use a less than doctoral level to get your points across. In fact, an interesting experience occurred in a sophisticated employee benefits company. The editor of their newsletter explained that she took over the job from a woman who was determined to write the newsletter for attorneys in "legalese." The former editor used the most long-winded expressions she could find, thinking that this was the manner in which attorneys wished to be addressed. When this new, enlightened editor took over the job, she wanted to make some changes. She told the staff to write their articles in "plain English."

The staff rebelled. They said that attorneys would never respect the information; they would think it an insult to their intelligence; the newsletter would never again be credible.

The new editor stood her ground. "Let's try it for one issue and see what happens," she told her staff. The results were amazing. The new editor reported that she received more thank-you letters and letters of praise for this particular issue than ever in her career. One attorney even wrote, "Thank you for writing to us in a very readable style. It was the most interesting newsletter we have ever received. Keep up the good work."

It is important to remember that reading level does not equate to education level in effective business writing. Regardless of the educational level of your audience, you still need to communicate to them in clear, simple, conversational English to be the most effective in your communications.

Government agencies are notorious for the amount of gobbledygook included per letter. The following simple paragraphs are full of overly abstract writing:

> *Poor:* There have been incidents wherein tort claims have been filed alleging that personal effects contained in seized vehicles have been lost or stolen while the vehicles were in our custody. Other problems have developed with seized merchandise being left in vehicles and the merchandise inadvertently being released when the vehicle is claimed by the owner/driver.
>
> Effective immediately the procedures contained herein will be utilized when a vehicle is seized or detained. Section 405 of the local Policies and Procedures Manual will be modified to reflect these guidelines. IBC Information Bulletin No. 14 has been superseded by the instructions contained herein.

To make these paragraphs more readable, you only need to simplify them:

> *Better:* Tort claims have been filed showing that personal property in seized vehicles has been lost or stolen while we were in charge of the vehicles. Other problems have occurred when seized merchandise is left inadvertently in the vehicle.

Effective immediately use the following procedures when a vehicle is seized or detained. We will modify Section 405 of the local policies and procedures manual to reflect these guidelines. These instructions will supersede the IBC Bulletin No. 14.

This revised letter excerpt is more concise and easily understood, regardless of the reader's education level.

Occupation. People speak various occupational languages, often called *jargon*. If, for example, the computer hardware engineers can't comprehend the jargon of the software analysts' suggestions, that means trouble. You may be a manager whose letters must go to different departments. What are you going to do to ensure that your writing gets through to everyone? Jargon can't do the job unless everybody understands it!

If you weren't an airline flight attendant, could you understand this information update, issued by the local labor union?

> *Poor:* The last two updates gave examples of violations of the 8 in 24-hour rule. Remember this is a rolling 24-hour period exclusive of deadhead, limo, duty rig, push back or tow in. The flight duty is termed "hard" flying and only the scheduled or rescheduled flight time is counted, *overflying is not included.*

The same philosophy applies to acronyms. How many times have you received a letter from a specific profession that is full of abbreviations which are familiar to members of that profession but unknown to you? Avoid letters like the following (from an engineer) if your audience is outside of your profession.

> *Poor:* Recently, the APB malfunctioned, causing a chain reaction among the TRQs, CEBs, and the APs.

Please, when using these machines, follow all instructions and make sure that all the machines
contain enough SOL, TONE, and RALDO to finish
your job. Have TLC with the machines! Thanks.

WHAT DO YOU WANT TO ACHIEVE?

The third and final question to ask and think about before you write a letter is: what action or actions should the reader take as a result of reading your letter? The action could be a decision or response, a resignation or vote, a donation, an appointment, a contract, a telephone call, etc.

Your business letters will ideally lead up to the result you desire the reader to take. If you are making a simple and common request, your request can be straightfor-ward. If the request is for something out of the ordinary or the circumstances are in some way complicated, you may need to be more persuasive in your arguments, your supporting evidence, or both.

In most cases you will need to explicitly state your request, since inferred and implicit requests may not be as clearly understood—or may be missed altogether! If your request is plausible, it often helps to provide a date for any action to take place. For example, when do you need to have a response, or when you will next call the reader?

Although some letters are written solely to inform, and do not require any action to be taken by the reader, most business letters require some type of response. If you are unable to determine what result you desire from your letter, maybe you should not be writing at all! Most of us, however, do communicate for specific purposes, and it's critical to keep that in mind before you begin to write. Most letters should lead up to and reinforce the desired action the writer wants the reader to take.

CHAPTER 2

Prewrite

BRAINSTORMING

MINDMAPPING

FREEWRITING

"Okay," you're thinking, "now I'm ready to write." You're probably also saying to yourself, "I've done all the preliminary work, determined my purpose, and researched my audience. Isn't it time to sketch a quick outline, write my letter, and stop?" The answer is "NO." Why not? Because the latest research on effective writing shows that the most important of all stages in your writing is what writing experts call "The Prewriting Stage."

Prewriting involves techniques for generating ideas and sorting them out. They are very different from the traditional outlining techniques you were taught in school. Outlining is a left-brain function. It attempts to organize ideas before you even come up with them. Prewriting is just the opposite. It taps into your right brain, which lets you creatively come up with ideas in a random, free-flowing fashion. It allows you a greater range of ideas and creativity than the traditional outlining structure ever permitted.

In this section we'll discuss prewriting techniques including:

○ Brainstorming

○ Mindmapping

○ Freewriting

These creative techniques will lead up to the development of a more formal organizational outline for your writing.

Briefly, brainstorming lets you free-associate your ideas in a random, unstructured form. Mindmapping, sometimes called clustering, allows you to group your topics in a creative, flowing diagram. Freewriting takes these ideas and lets you write them all out without stopping, censoring, editing, or starting over. You'll soon see examples of all three.

Finally, organizing lets you take the free-flowing ideas you've created by brainstorming, mindmapping, and freewriting, and put them in a meaningful, powerful order so you can begin to write with direction.

All of these techniques are superior to traditional outlining, which assumes you know the order of ideas before you even have them.

BRAINSTORMING

The director of a large hospital planned to give his organization's public relations manager information about a promotion he'd just received. He was excited about his job change but had buried his enthusiasm in a bland, routinely written letter. Luckily, he happened to be in one of our writing classes and brought the completed letter with him. "I know it isn't very interesting," he admitted, "but it's the best I could do. I struggled with it for hours." His letter read like this:

> *Poor:* This is to inform you that effective October 1, 1989, I have accepted the position of Corporate Vice President, Business & Industry Division of Health Services, Inc. In this capacity, my duties will include developing a new division which will be responsible

for the marketing and sales of all existing services
within the corporation and both hospitals, and the
creation of industrial programs.

When he learned that brainstorming is the key to
creative letters, his eyes brightened. He energetically wrote
down all his ideas on the topic, nonstop. This is exactly
what brainstorming is about. Fifteen minutes later he had
dashed off 20 thoughts. He recognized that once he un-
locked his creativity, he could transform even the most
mundane topic into an eye-catching, fascinating piece of
writing. Eventually he revised his letter.

First he brainstormed it:

1. Promotion

2. New opportunities selling new products

3. Giving new opportunities new markets—
   giving out free samples

4. Expanding old ideas—quotas, rewards, hospital relations

5. Sales incentives
   new industries
   new people
   cutting edge of technology
   vacations for good sales
   higher wages

Then he rewrote it:

Better: I will be accepting the position of Corporate
Vice President, Business and Industry Division,
Health Services, Inc. on October 1, 1989. With my
new position I will be able to create new opportunities, provide greater sales incentives, and establish
different markets. In addition, I will be responsible

> for developing a new division, consisting of market-
> ing and sales within the corporation and both hospi-
> tals. Plus, I will create new industrial programs.

His reactions on this new learning: "I always thought I had to delegate all my writing to someone else. Deep down I was sure about the strength of my ideas—I just didn't know how to get them out!" He added, "Now I feel like a 'reborn writer'!"

You can brainstorm as effectively as he did. Here are steps to help you to brainstorm the simplest letter to the most complex piece of writing. Start by jotting down one insight after another about your topic.

While you're doing this, imagine that you're a reporter holding fast to your five sacred W's and one H:

- ○ WHO (will receive it, does it affect)?
- ○ WHAT (is it about)?
- ○ WHY (is it needed)?
- ○ WHERE (will it occur)?
- ○ WHEN (are its deadlines scheduled)?
- ○ HOW (will it be carried out)?

Then get going! Generate as many ideas as you can on your topic. The important point here is that you do no editing at all. An inner voice might shout, "No!" or "That's ridiculous!" or "You already said that!" Ignore it. This is your time to be completely creative and uncensored. You'll have plenty of opportunities to edit and polish. This is like summer vacation—no school rules; have fun!

The manager of a telecommunications firm had to write a letter about sick leave benefits. He was stuck—he tried to turn out a polished product before he even began.

Out of frustration, he decided to brainstorm. He soon became excited, conjuring up many more interesting aspects of the issue than he had ever imagined, simply because he took the time to brainstorm!

The manager forgot about the finished product. All he wanted was to put his concepts on paper. Afterwards he admitted his amazement at how many thoughts he had on the subject. By trying to get the letter completed quickly, he felt cut off from his thoughts. But when he allowed his mind to flow freely in the right-brain mode, he found that his personal resources were richer than he ever expected. People who write like this are relieved to discover how much they have to say. No longer does the composition process block or limit them.

BRAINSTORMING

○ Stress quantity, not quality of ideas

○ Encourage "piggyback" and add-on ideas

○ No editing or evaluation

○ Make it fun!

MINDMAPPING

A close cousin to brainstorming is a technique called mindmapping. Mindmapping relaxes the usual rigidity of writing. It is a visual representation of the way your mind sorts information. You start with your central idea in the center of your page, then branch your ideas off this core idea. Sometimes mindmapping is called "clustering" because the mind clusters, or lumps, related ideas. The mind doesn't sort information in big and little "A's" or in roman numerals I and II as does an outline. Outlining often gets in the way of creativity rather than promoting it. Mindmapping does the opposite. It follows your mental process and encourages creativity.

There is no one correct way to mindmap, but here are some general guidelines to get you started.

- In the center of your paper, draw a square or a circle.

- Inside it, write the name of your project, subject of your correspondence, or item you discuss.

- Draw branches from the circle, like branches from a tree, to designate your main topics or concerns.

- To help identify these topics, you might use the 5W's and 1H. Ask yourself who, what, why, where, when, and how.

- Branch off into smaller but related topics.

- Don't worry about the organization of your branches; that comes later.

- Use different colored pens or pencils to designate related topics.

A group of police officers learning report writing from us were attentive but still unexcited about writing. Then they learned about mindmapping! They picked up their pens and began to apply the technique to their report writing forms. One officer produced the following on his first attempt:

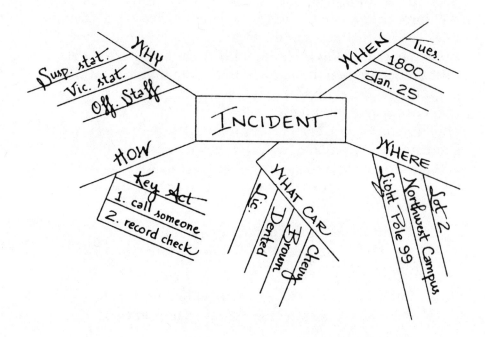

He and his colleagues were excited about this technique. They said it would help them organize and energize their report writing. It can do the same for you!

After you've brainstormed or mindmapped, you may have a few final flashes of insight for your letter.

Remember, your brainstorming and mindmapping generate the basic building blocks of your letter. They provide the skeleton, or the framework, of your subject. Once you're finished with them, much of your work is finished.

But what if you can't think of any ideas? If that happens, and it often does, simply write something down—anything, even if it's unrelated to your subject. Your brain will enjoy this kind of freedom. Once you get in the groove again, your brainstorms, mindmaps, and freewriting will take off. Suddenly, you'll look down at your ideas, and they will have multiplied.

I remember an engineer we worked with on his reports. He claimed that the things he wrote were so routine and unimaginative that the thought of writing bored him unbearably. But once he started brainstorming, he got new angles that enabled him to look forward to this previously dreaded task. At the end of our seminar, he said, "Hey, brainstorming is the best tool I've ever been taught for writing. I don't worry about being blocked anymore. Now I know where and how to get going again. Thanks a lot."

MINDMAPPING

○ Start with your general topic

○ Extend lines as ideas relate to the topic

○ Branch out from subtopics as necessary

○ Don't worry about organization

○ Use different colors or letters to designate related topics

FREEWRITING

A third prewriting technique to loosen you up and start you off is known as freewriting. The key to freewriting is writing without an editor, that is, a voice that instructs you to edit, change, and rewrite as you compose. To freewrite, pick up your pen or start your word processor and begin composing, without making any changes, corrections, or starting over. Ignore punctuation, spelling, grammar, and organization. Let your thoughts flow freely. You'll have time later to go back and revise them. In freewriting, your mind may wander to next month's golf tournament or tonight's dinner. Don't worry about it, just write. Here's an example of one client's freewriting.

FREEWRITING SAMPLE:

let's see . . . gotta talk about sales projections and etc. I need letters from you, Sandy, Jim about sales projections for the following quarter and related supporting info. Also need you to think about profit sharing (Does that include a trip to Mexico?). Got to inform employees about benefits, dental, medical, vacations—incorporate *their* ideas. Need a meeting next week.

REVISED:

Joe, let's call a meeting of all managers next Tuesday and discuss sales projections for the following quarter. Before the meeting we'll need input from you, Sandy, and Jim on your own projections. We also need to think about our profit-sharing fund and to let the employees know about their benefits. How about getting together Monday to discuss all of the above?

Sometimes it's easier to freewrite after you've brainstormed or mindmapped. You have your ideas; then use each topic to produce sentences, then paragraphs, then your letter! Don't worry about your form, formats, overall look. Just keep writing as quickly and freely as you can.

Most people say it's easier to edit than to write. So, once you have your rough draft, you can then go back and clean it up. But the hard part's over; you have your copy.

FREEWRITING

○ Write without stopping

○ Create without editing

○ Double-spaced format

○ Allow no criticizing

○ Let it sit!

CHAPTER 3

ORGANIZE

Okay, now you're finished with brainstorms, mindmaps, and freewriting. You've come up with your ideas on your topic. But you may say, "What will I do with all these? All I need to produce is a one-page letter."

You've done the groundwork; you need to organize your brainstorms, mindmaps, and freewriting to get to a final draft. You're going to begin to determine which ideas stay and which ones go. We don't suggest a big red pen or a giant pair of scissors. We do, however, recommend a system of ordering. Number your thoughts in order of importance—to whom? To your reader of course!

Disorganized letters are hazardous. The real problem with poor organization is that it creates unnecessary length—just what you don't want. Think about the best letter you've ever received. Was it:

- ○ Long or short?
- ○ Rambling or direct?
- ○ Scrambled or organized?
- ○ Muddy or clear?

You probably answered those questions without even thinking. There's no mystery to good writing. Just make your letters short, direct, organized, and clear. And stop! Curiously, the mark of punctuation that people too seldom use is the period. They want to ramble when they need to STOP! Use the period!

Once you have all the information and ideas that you want to communicate listed on paper, you need to consider how best to sequence your thoughts. Your method of sequencing should have a logical flow to be most effective.

ORGANIZING YOUR PREWRITING

You can organize your prewriting ideas simply by numbering your initial recorded thoughts. For example, look at the following mindmap.

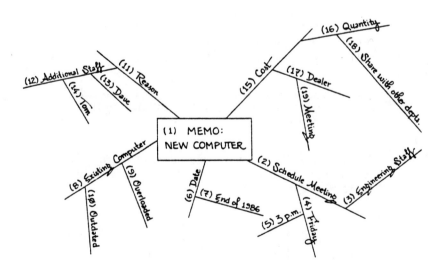

Notice the numbers next to each topic. We've prioritized the topics in the order we felt best for the reader. By numbering your brainstorms or the branches of your maps, you can decide which topics are the most important. You can use these subjects as headers, which we will discuss later, when you actually begin to write your letter.

When you write, go directly to your primary point; your best organizational guidelines for brief letters contain these characteristics:

○ One to three main points, arranged with the most important point first

○ Several examples to support each point

○ One or two comments on each example

Example:

> We need to make three major budget cuts. The first will be cutting back on foreign investments. The dollar is not strong now. It can do better domestically.

> Second, we will decrease foreign services because of our slowdown in investments. This will free up money to invest elsewhere.

> Finally, we will cut back on foreign travel. Since our foreign investments will diminish, we shouldn't have to travel as extensively.

Although there are many ways information can be organized, we will concentrate on three methods that are the most common and effective in business letters—namely, chronological, problem-solving (or cause-and-effect), and decreasing order of importance.

CHRONOLOGICAL ORGANIZATION

In a chronological format of organizing information, you arrange your thoughts in the order in which events you are discussing occurred, beginning with the first event. This is an effective means for presenting information in many business letters, since business letters often refer to events that have occurred in a sequence or to a series of actions. A chronological format can also be used when you need to be descriptive, such as for trip reports, work schedules, minutes of meetings, and accident reports.

Note that the organization of the letter on pages 32–33 follows the sequence of events as they occured. This letter follows a chronological sequence because it is the most logical way to present the information.

CHRONOLOGICAL ORGANIZATION FORMAT

- ○ Overview
- ○ State series of events in the order in which they occurred
- ○ Give explanation, as necessary
- ○ Conclusion

9993 Avenida Magnifica
San Diego, CA 92131

June 22, 19XX

Mr. W. Graham Claytor, Jr.
President
AMTRACK
400 North Capitol Street NW
Washington, DC 20001

Dear Mr. Claytor:

Do you wonder why so few Americans consider the
railroad as a viable means of transportation? Here's
a recent experience I had:

I needed to travel from Oakland to Sacramento, CA
last Saturday, and although I hadn't ridden Amtrack
for nine years, I thought: "I bet that would be a
beautiful and enjoyable train trip." So I bought a
ticket on your rail.

My reservation was for 12:30 p.m., and since Oakland is a one-rail track and I was carrying my bag on
board, I pulled into the station at 12:15, with a
comment to my driver: "perfect timing." I was quite
surprised to find the train pulling out as I entered
the building moments later.

When I approached the ticket clerk, a Mr. J. Smith,
to inquire why the train was leaving early, he
proceeded—with a broad grin—to lecture me that
"12:30 was no time to check in for a 12:30 departure." I agreed, and said that that was why I was
here at (what was now) 12:19. He immediately said
my travel agent made a mistake, although a woman
next to me had a ticket with the same time that she
had purchased only the morning before. He took my
ticket, gave it to the other clerk, who gave it to this
other woman at the next window because he thought
we were traveling together. (I didn't know her, nor
did I see what was happening to my ticket.)

It turns out that for some reason (clearly none
pertaining to customer convenience) the schedule
had been moved up by 10 minutes some five weeks
earlier! The clerk unconvincingly explained to me
that attempts were made to call everyone. (There is

Mr. Graham Clayton, Jr.
June 22, 19XX
Page 2

always a person or an answering service at my phone
number.) The clerks then suggested we try to catch
the train at the next stop, which they claimed was 30
minutes away. This woman I didn't know offered to
take me. When I asked for my ticket back, I was told
it had been returned to me. I had to repeatedly insist
that it had not.

It took 45 minutes to reach the next station in Mar-
tinez, CA, where we found five to six people milling
behind the counter. The train was long gone, only
now we were in a small town without even a bus
station. When I commented on the early departure of
the train, the consensus from behind the counter
was that the train could not have left early because
"that was against the law." You can imagine how
comforting this was to me!

After a wild ride to another town, we found a bus
station and caught a bus. The other woman had to
take a 17-hour bus ride to Salt Lake City. I arrived in
Sacramento harried and upset.

So that's my story. My pleasurable ride on Amtrack
became a living nightmare, in large part because
your rail has little or no interest in providing quality
customer service. There are many, many things that
any of your employees could have done along the way
to assist or comfort me, yet I saw little effort to do so.
It will probably be another nine years before I'm able
to forget this experience and try Amtrack again—if
then.

Sincerely,

Robert B. Nelson

p.s.: Do yourself and your company a favor and get a
copy of *Moments of Truth* by Jan Carlzon. It explains
how he, the president of SAS, turned that European
airline around, largely through attention to customers and customer interactions.

PROBLEM-SOLVING/CAUSE-AND-EFFECT ORGANIZATION

A second common format for organizing information in a business letter is a problem-solving or cause-and-effect format. This format is used to address a problem situation and its planned resolution, or to explain why certain events caused other events to happen. For example, if you were trying to explain why absenteeism was on the increase in your department, you would use a problem-solving or cause-and-effect analysis. In this case, you would be working from an effect by first citing the problem (higher absenteeism rate) and then its probable cause (lower morale, nonexistent or noncommunicated policies, poor enforcement of absenteeism policies, and so on).

If, on the other hand, your purpose was to analyze the possible effects of a proposed change, such as a new benefits package for employees, you would also use cause-and-effect analysis, only this time, you would start with the cause (proposed benefits changes) and look for possible effects that would logically follow (cost to the company, improvements in worker morale and retention, and so on).

The goal of problem-solving or cause-and-effect analysis is to make the relationship between a situation and either its cause or its effect as logical, easy-to-understand, and plausible as possible. The conclusions you draw about the relationship will be based on the facts and data that you report. For this reason, the selection of data to support your arguments is of vital importance and will directly affect how convincing your communication will be. Following are three guidelines we recommend for selecting data to use in your letters: data should be factual, data should be relevant, and data should logically follow.

DATA SHOULD BE FACTUAL.   Information to back up your points should be as factual as possible to give your arguments credibility. If something is known to be true, state the fact and give the source of the information. "Budget expenditures exceeded forecast for FY 1988 by 12 percent, according to the company's annual report," is a statement of fact with a supporting source. "Most employees in this company dislike the new cafeteria," is a statement of fact only if it can be better quantified and validated—otherwise the statement could be based on hearsay. Good writing always has a basis in truth.

DATA SHOULD BE RELEVANT.   Even if the data you present is accurate, you should be careful not to draw conclusions that the data doesn't support. You may have some survey information, for example, that indicates that an increasing number of employees are satisfied with their jobs at your company. But you cannot use this information as evidence that they are unconcerned about career opportunities and their promotion potential. The two points are unrelated unless specifically linked in the survey. It is better to refer to specific items in the survey that directly relate to career opportunities and promotion potential, rather than try to make any assumptions that are based on loosely related information in the survey.

DATA SHOULD LOGICALLY FOLLOW.   Two events that occur close to each other in time or place may or may not be casually related. Sales may have improved during the month that annual bonuses were announced, but chances are there is no connection between the two events. In order to determine just what improved sales, you should consider all relevant factors, such as recent changes in advertising, special promotions, sales incentives, or lower prices. You must then demonstrate the relationship with pertinent facts and arguments. Often it is difficult to determine which factors directly caused a particular event. For example, it might be difficult to determine whether increased sales incentives or lower prices contributed more toward improving sales. If this is the case, then you should report your findings as objectively as possible and present your conclusions as possible explanations — not facts.

PROBLEM-SOLVING APPROACH
(Cause-and-Effect)

1. Define problem
   (who-what-where-when-why-how)

2. Define solution
   (statement)

3. Evaluate solution
   (list premises)

CAUSE-AND-EFFECT
(Example Argument)

Statement	Rail line from Twin Cities to Seattle should not be abandoned
Premise 1	800 railroad employees will lose jobs
Premise 2	There will be increased gasoline usage and air pollution
Premise 3	125 companies will relocate to other states

ORGANIZATION BY DECREASING ORDER OF IMPORTANCE

Fiction often builds up suspense; it makes you wait for the climax. Good business writing does just the opposite; it opens with the most important information and tapers off to the least important. The "bottom line" becomes the top line. When you organize your information according to a decreasing order of importance, you begin with the most important fact or point, then go on to the next most important and so on, ending with the least important information or fact. This is the method of writing used by most newspapers. The most significant information always appears first in a news story, with related, secondary information and more details of the events completing the story.

This method of presenting information is effective and highly appreciated in business, in that it gives the reader needed information fast. Readers will not have to hunt through your letter to find the most important or relevant facts of the situation; they will trust that you have done this for them.

The foundation of this method of organizing is the principle of *inductive* reasoning. Simply stated, your conclusion comes first. Next, you explain how you arrived at your conclusion and why you support it. The opposite of inductive reasoning is *deductive* reasoning, which leaves the most important for last, building toward some kind of climax. While deductive reasoning might work well in a novel, it is not that effective in a business letter. It muddies the communication, and it wastes the time of your busy colleagues and clients. To write inductively:

○ Put your most important point up front.

○ Focus your audience's attention on it.

○ Explain it extensively.

○ Support and develop it strongly.

Whatever you do to emphasize your most important point, the opening of your letter will contain more substance than the close. If you paid six dollars to see a movie, you'd be furious if you knew the ending within the first five minutes. But if you had only five minutes to read an important letter, you'd be amazed if you couldn't find the facts right away.

A bank executive flew in from Santa Barbara to consult with us about her writing. She was concerned about a letter to her colleague that discussed the print size on the colleague's training slides. After reading two pages of background information, justification, and reasoning, we began to wonder, "When is she going to get to the point?"

Finally, buried in page three, she wrote, "I think the typeface should be larger on the slides to make them easier to read." Why didn't she put this in the beginning? She explained that she thought she had to build up to her request and lead her reader slowly to the main point.

When we asked her if that's what she wants when she receives a letter, she responded, "No! I want them to get to the point right away and not waste my time!" Without any further explanation, she smiled and started her letter with her request. Be bold!

A hotel supervisor once asked, "But what if I'm asking for something that I know my reader doesn't want to give me—like a special parking spot, a day off, or the use of a company car for a day?" In such cases, and in cases where you're writing "negative" or "bad news" letters, it's best not to start the letter off immediately with the request. Instead, begin with a single logical reason that prepares the reader.

For example:

> Because I work the late shift, I don't arrive until
> 4 p.m. By this time, all the company parking spaces
> are still full from the previous shift. Would you
> designate some spaces where parking is limited from
> 9–4, leaving them open for second shift employees?

But in most cases, organize your letters like journalists do, with the most important information up front. That's the critical difference between writing for information (inductive writing) and writing for entertainment (deductive writing). After you've completed your draft, find the most important information, circle it, and put it as close to the beginning of your letter as you can.

When you write, think about the one sentence you would keep if you could save only one. Put that sentence right up front—if it's not your first sentence (and often it can be), then it certainly belongs in your first paragraph. Remember these letter tips, and your letters will get the point across quickly and clearly. Put:

- ○ Good news before bad news
- ○ Requests before justifications
- ○ Answers before explanations
- ○ Conclusions before discussions
- ○ Summaries before details
- ○ Generalities before specifics

GOOD BUSINESS WRITING IS NO MYSTERY!

ORGANIZATION

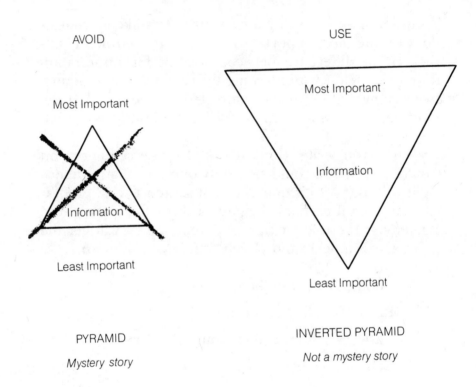

CHAPTER 4

Outline

OPENING

MIDDLE OR BODY

CLOSING

All our discussion about planning what to say in letters leads up to the very fundamental — and important — step of outlining. All good writing has an outline at its core. An outline is simply a map for where you are going. It helps to keep you on track to achieve the purpose of your communication. Outlines do not need to be overly detailed; in fact, we often use only three to five key words for one-page business letters.

In this section we will discuss the parts and types of letters, and show how they can be used to organize typical business correspondence. A simple yet effective way to outline is to think of the standard parts common to all letters — namely, the opening, body, and closing.

OPENING

A well-known writer once said that people most remember the material they read first and last. What comes in between is important, but it doesn't stick with readers the way beginnings and endings do. The first paragraph of your correspondence is the most powerful part of your letter. The first paragraph of a business letter should accomplish the following three things:

○ Grab the reader's attention.

○ Get directly to the point.

○ Set a professional and courteous tone.

When the beginning paragraph is direct and interesting, the recipient will read the entire letter with care. If the paragraph rambles or is unclear, the reader may skim or even skip the rest of the letter. So make that first paragraph effective by observing these three principles:

○ Make it short.

○ Say something concrete.

○ Entice your audience.

Keep your first paragraph to two or three short sentences. You're more likely to keep your reader involved in what you write. There's nothing more discouraging to a busy individual than facing a long page of lengthy sentences and paragraphs.

Ensure that your paragraph really *says* something by avoiding all unnecessary preliminaries and getting to your message fast. Too many writers waste the most important part of their letter — the first paragraph — telling the reader that his or her letter has been received or that it was dated March 10. They mistakenly use this paragraph as a warm-up exercise instead of addressing the business at hand.

> *Poor:* We are in receipt of your letter dated April 4, informing us of a mistake we made in filling your last order. We appreciate your calling our attention to the problem and we are taking steps to rectify the situation.

Better: Thank you for your letter about our mistake in filling your last order. We've corrected the error. You should receive your order by next Monday.

The opening captures the reader's attention. In general, you want to write business letters that come to the point and do not spend excessive time building up to those points or rehashing previous correspondence. Good letter openings are brief, similar to openings in one-on-one conversations. Avoid overused openings such as: "In response to your letter of . . ." or "We are in receipt of your recent letter regarding. . . ." Such passive phrases will drain your letters of freshness and energy and make it more difficult to communicate clearly.

Letter openings vary according to the purpose of the letter. In general, when you have good news to give the reader, you should do it right away. If you have bad news to give to the reader, it is often best to soften the bad news by first saying something that is positive. And if the letter is seeking to be persuasive, you need to begin by grabbing the reader's attention and drawing him or her into the letter.

MIDDLE OR BODY

The body of your letter presents the bulk of the information you are trying to communicate. How it is organized depends upon the purpose of your letter. In the last section we discussed the most common ways to organize the body of business letters: chronological, problem-solving, and decreasing order of importance. The discussion of the body of the letter makes up most of the subsequent chapters of this book.

CLOSING

There are many different types of business letters. Some letters inform while others request. Some complain while others praise. The majority of them, however, *ask* the recipient for something, directly or indirectly. Whether the writer wants a contribution to a cause or a refund for a faulty product, the clearer and stronger the message is, the more likely it will get a response.

The closing of your letters should typically seek to encourage the reader to take some specific action such as making a decision, forwarding a reply, or correcting a problem. In many ways the closing of a letter parallels the opening. Both should be short, to the point, and specific. Both should be free of overused, passive phrases that do not communicate much (such as "thanking you in advance . . .")

Whenever possible your letters should specifically state what action is expected of the reader and by when. This dated action increases the chances that your reader will respond as requested.

The question, "Why am I writing this?" will help you determine what type of call to action you need at the end of your correspondence. This call to action is critical to your letter.

It's also important to let your reader know when to take action. A simple "Please call me by next Tuesday with your answer" may be all that's needed to secure the response you want.

When you finish what you want to say, stop. Many people feel compelled at the end of a letter to add routine phrases like, "If you have any questions please call," or "I hope this answers your question," or "Please give this matter your careful consideration." Avoid these familiar platitudes which sound neither sincere nor friendly and are overused and tired. Unless you have other important topics to discuss, just end your letter with a simple call to action and your signature. If there is nothing more to say, simply end the letter — do not feel it is necessary to ramble on about unrelated or personal topics.

A personal touch to your letter can be effective, but be certain it's in good taste. If you really don't know the person this won't work, but if you are on more familiar terms, notes like the following are welcome: "Sorry to hear you've been ill. Hope you're feeling better," or "Congratulations on winning the top sales award. You deserve it."

It is important to keep your closing paragraph in the same tone as the letter. We suggest using the simple, always acceptable "Sincerely." Closings like "Very truly yours," or "Warmest regards" are outdated.

CHAPTER 5

PLAN IT: REFERENCE MATERIAL AND EXERCISES

FORMATTING YOUR BUSINESS LETTERS

QUIZ: INSIDE ADDRESSES AND LETTER SALUTATIONS

WHAT IF YOU DICTATE?

SOME BASIC RULES OF PUNCTUATION FOR BUSINESS WRITING

FORMATTING YOUR BUSINESS LETTERS

The appearance of your letter is an important part of the overall professional image you communicate to your readers. This appearance is determined by the letter's style, letterhead stationery, and format.

LETTER STYLE

If your company has a standard format, follow it. If not, we suggest block style, the same style we recommend for memos. It's cleaner and easier to read. Letters, like memos, should be single-spaced, double-spaced between paragraphs, left-justified, and ragged right (that is, an uneven right margin as is common in typed letters). An alternative acceptable format is to indent the beginning of each paragraph.

The most important issue is consistency, especially when you correspond frequently with the same outside agency or client. Here is an example of a block style letter:

April 3, 19XX

Mr. Steven McDonald, President
Computer Applications Incorporated
2500 Industrial Drive
North Hollywood, CA 91330

Reference: CBT Training Program

Dear Steve:

As you requested during our meeting of February 23, 19XX, I have enclosed the following materials:

○ A copy of the revised contract

○ A copy of the initial proposal

○ A sample of our Alphawriter Training Manual

I look forward to working with you. Please call me if you have any questions.

Sincerely,

Marianne P. Floyd
Assistant Vice President
ABC Computer Company

cc: J. Bealstein
    R. Roberts

LETTERHEAD STATIONERY

The quality of your paper and the type of letterhead project your company's image. You probably already have good quality paper and a standard letterhead. If yours is a small company, or you've just gone into business for yourself, one of the first things you must do is to invest in printing your letterhead. Use high-quality bond paper with matching printed envelopes. The letterhead may include any symbol or emblem (called a logo) that identifies or describes your company. It is typically centered on the top of the stationery. It should also include the following:

○ Name of your company. The name of your company should tell what you do. If it doesn't, it's fine to add a descriptive phrase that provides this information. For example, if your company is an accounting firm, and you call yourself The TM Company of Chicago, you could add the phrase, "Tax Accounting and Auditing" beneath the company name.

○ Location. This should include your address or P.O. box, telephone number, and telex or telefax number.

○ Simplicity. Don't clutter your stationery. Remember, the more white space on a page, the easier it is to read and the more attractive it looks.

○ Optional descriptive information. This can include officers and partners. Just don't include excessive information.

STANDARD BUSINESS LETTER FORMAT

While there are many different letter types, most business letters have a similar format, that is, a standard layout followed throughout business. This standard format allows writers and readers to save time and avoid confusion by having a common reference for different items of a business letter.

Some companies even provide employees with exact letter formats for all company correspondence. Such guidelines can help make your job easier. In addition, they create a classy look for all corporate communication. When you create a unified appearance for your business writing, you are more apt to create a professional image that can enhance your business. Following is a standard business letter and a corresponding discussion that refers to each of the numbered sections.

(1) April 14, 19XX

(2) Mr. Marshall Hall
Vice President of Operations
ABC Construction Co., Inc.
5849 Ocean Way
San Diego, CA 92101

(3) Attention: (not needed in this letter)

(4) Reference: Job #8500

(5) Subject: CHANGES IN OUR
INVOICING PROCEDURES

(6) Dear Sam:

(7) Thanks for making the First Ocean Way Condominium project a success. So that you can receive payments on time, we have decided to change our billing procedures. Proper use of the new system will encourage faster payment.

Let me briefly list the new procedures that will affect San Diego Construction:

(8) ○ Send all invoices to the proper ABC Division

○ Continue to send construction warranty invoices to the ABC Company P.O. Box.

○ Obtain a work order number from Joseph Kychik (619) 555-5000 before you begin any warranty work.

○ List warranty work order numbers on time sheets, equipment sheets, and material invoices.

Our accounting department informed me today that it will return any invoices received for work performed on or after April 13, 19XX, unless the warranty work order numbers appear on the face of the invoice.

(9) I look forward to working with you again in the near future.

(10) Mr. Marshall Hall
ABC Construction Company
Page 2

(11) Sincerely,

(12) Barbara A. Francis
Project Manager
ABC Company

(13) JAL/jss

(14) Enclosures

(15) cc: P. Hardy
M. Floyd
J. Forbes

(16) p.s.:

1. Date. The date is the first item to be written, typically in the form of the month (spelled out), day, and year (both as numerals).

In the modern block format that we advocate for business letters, the date is flush left as are all other items in the letter. (In a modified block format the date, as well as the closing, is indented to about half way across the page.)

Allow four line spaces before the beginning of your inside address.

2. Inside Address. This is the name and address of the person or group you are writing to. Whenever possible, address your letters to a specific person and put that individual's name on the first line of the inside address, followed by their title, department, and company name, each on subsequent lines.

After the company name, which may be placed in all capital letters, the street address is on the next line, followed by the city, state, and zip code. If you are not writing to a specific person, the first line of the inside address should be the company's name, followed by the department name.

If a post office box is used, it should be placed on a line by itself directly above the city/state/zip line. Avoid abbreviations in the inside address (as well as throughout your business correspondence), whenever possible. Exceptions: Mr., Mrs., Ms., SW, NE.

Crucial to the success of your correspondence is to write the recipient's name and title correctly. If you don't, you may unintentionally offend your reader before he or she even gets to your first paragraph. Since names and titles change rapidly in business today, you need to be on guard for dated references. Usually a quick phone call is enough to verify the correct spelling of a name and the person's current title. Also, if you're writing to a woman, ask if she goes by Mrs., Ms., or Miss. Details like that *do* make a difference in how your correspondence is received.

3. Attention Line. Although once very popular in business writing, attention lines are seldom used today, and you should avoid using them. In the past, all business letters were addressed to a company with an attention line to an individual within the company. We recommend simply addressing the letter to the individual to whom you are writing.

4. Reference. The reference line often refers to job numbers, dates of previous meetings, or other material the writer needs to document. This line can take the place of repetitious, statistical information ("This letter concerns our July 12 meeting") that appears in the first line of a letter.

5. Subject Line. The first step toward helping the reader is to identify, whenever possible, the subject of your letter at the beginning of the letter. This is done with the subject line. The subject line should be specific, concise, and appealing. It should grab your reader's attention — after all, you want to get your letter noticed.

For example, rather than using, "Subject: Vendor Review," try something more to the heart of the matter like, "Subject: Vender Service Contract Review," or "Subject: Year-End Service Contract Review." Be as specific and active as possible when you indicate your subject and try to include a verb.

If you are unsure of your subject, you're not yet ready to write your letter. To help identify your subject, review your initial questions once again:

○ Why am I writing this letter?

○ Who will be reading it?

○ What do I hope to accomplish?

Keep the answers to these questions in mind as you write your letter. The following letter has a subject line and opening sentence that leaves no doubt about the subject matter of the letter:

> Subject: Revision of Self-Employed Keogh Plan Rules
>
> Dear ABC S & L Retirement Accountholders:
>
> Your telephone calls indicate that our rules and regulations on your retirement account are unclear.
>
> In this letter we will try to simplify these rules.

The letter goes on to explain in detail the various accounts, addressing some of the specific questions the savings and loan received.

6. *Salutation.* This is the formal greeting of the letter, which should correspond in gender and number with the top line of the inside address. Thus, a letter to "Mr. John

Smith" would have a salutation of "Dear Mr. Smith:"; a letter addressed to a company would have a plural salutation since a company consists of a group of people.

Make your salutation personal if you know the reader well. Instead of "Dear Sir" or "Dear Mr. Hall," use "Dear (first name)." Avoid impersonal and disinterested salutations such as "Gentlemen," "Dear Sir or Madam" or "To Whom it May Concern."

Your letter will be more effective if it is personally addressed to the recipient. Thus, whenever possible, find out the name of the person to whom you are writing. If you write a sales letter, take the time to find out the names of your clients. If you apply for a job, learn the name of the person whom you want to hire you. If you do, you'll increase your chances of getting an interview. If you bid on (or for) a contract, find out the names of the people who will award it.

If you can't find out an individual's name, address the person by the title of his or her position, such as: "Dear Personnel Manager," "Dear Alumni Association President," or "Dear Office Manager."

An alternate modern format—frequently used with computer-generated letters—omits the salutation and closing altogether.

The salutation is always followed by a colon in business correspondence (and by a comma in personal correspondence).

7. Opening Paragraph. Keep your first paragraph clear of references to previous correspondence and overused phrases. Instead, come directly to the point.

8. Body. This contains the message of your letter. Use lists as often as you can. This technique allows the reader to grasp the important points quickly.

Single-space the contents of your letter and double-space between paragraphs (unless you are indenting paragraphs). Try not to make your letters longer than one page. If this is not feasible, two pages should be the maximum length.

9. Closing Paragraph. The closing paragraph is a brief summary and thank you as appropriate. Avoid cliche-filled phrases such as "If you have any questions, please don't hesitate to call." Don't tell people to call you unless you want to hear from them. If you do want them to call, leave your number and an extension, especially if it's different from the one on your letterhead.

If you don't want the person to call, use statements such as "This letter should answer all your questions," or "I trust this information clarifies your questions." This approach closes the issue and discourages phone calls. We will discuss this part of your letter in greater detail later in this book.

10. Second Page Heading. If your letter is longer than one page, place the addressee at the top left of the second page, followed by the date and page number on subsequent lines. Space down about four lines, and begin your new paragraph. If possible, break your pages between paragraphs instead of within a paragraph.

11. Closing. The end of the letter traditionally has a closing. We advocate the use of "Sincerely" as a traditional closing. Other possibilities include, "Yours truly," "Regards," and "Very truly yours." Avoid being overly friendly with closings such as "Warmest regards," "Our sincere regards," or "Best wishes." Make the closing fit the nature of the relationship. If you aren't "very truly theirs" don't say it!

The closing is followed by a comma. If the closing is more than a single word, subsequent words are not capitalized.

12. Signature. Place the typed signature four spaces below the closing, aligned with the left margin. Place your title on the line directly below your name. The four spaces allow plenty of room for your signature. Sign every letter you write. If you are not available, and it's urgent that the letter go out, it's permissible to have someone else sign for you and place their initials next to your signature.

In this letter, we've placed the company name underneath Barbara's name and title. This practice is open to preference. If you have a company logo and letterhead, it might seem redundant. However, some large companies prefer to indicate the company's name at the end of the letter, especially if the letter is contractual in nature.

13. Writer/Typist. Upper case initials indicate the writer of the letter, and the lower case initials indicate the typist or the word processor.

14. Enclosures. Indicate "Enclosures" or "Attachments" on the line below the initials. Some writers prefer to specifically list the enclosures for clarity.

15. Carbon Copies. The "cc" is the acceptable abbreviation for people who receive copies of your letter. In this case, several people will receive a copy of this letter. Three are from ABC Construction Company. We advocate alphabetically listing the "cc" receivers.

16. Postscript. Some writers—especially with sales letters—add "p.s." to call attention to a certain item or to make the letter seem more informal. We prefer using "p.s." sparingly, if at all. It should not appear as if you had afterthoughts once you finished writing your letter. Any important points should be clearly stated in the body of your letter.

QUIZ: INSIDE ADDRESSES AND LETTER SALUTATIONS

Here's a fun little quiz on some of the things we just discussed (and a few things we haven't yet mentioned!) about inside addresses and salutations. Place a "T" for True or an "F" for False in the space provided. Answers immediately follow the quiz.

_____ 1. It's acceptable to use a person's first name in the salutation if you have met the person.

_____ 2. When both a street address and a post office box number are given, you should use the street address.

_____ 3. If the letterhead reads "Cubic Incorporated," you may address your letter "Cubic, Inc."

_____ 4. A comma always precedes "Inc." in an address.

_____ 5. The inside address should never exceed five lines.

_____ 6. In the inside address, the addressee's title should always appear on the line beneath his or her name.

_____ 7. It's acceptable to address a letter to "L.A., Calif." since many people refer to Los Angeles that way.

_____ 8. A letter addressed to a company, with an attention line to an individual, would have the salutation "Dear Mr. Blank."

_____ 9. The date of a letter should be centered under the letterhead, if the stationery has a letterhead.

_____ 10. A letter addressed to a woman would have the salutation "Dear Madam."

_____ 11. If the letter you are answering was signed with a first name which could be either sex, you can assume the writer is a man.

_____ 12. If you do not know a woman's marital status, you may address your letter "Ms. Mary Brown."

_____ 13. Streets and avenues whose names are actually numbers should be spelled out.

_____ 14. It's acceptable to use abbreviations in the body of a business letter.

_____ 15. If a business letter is addressed to someone's home, it should be marked "Personal."

_____ 16. It is acceptable to have the day precede the month in the date line of business correspondence (as in 3 August, 19XX).

_____ 17. If a man has a degree he should be addressed as Dr. James Rogers, Ph.D.

_____ 18. The honorary titles Honorable and Reverend are usually abbreviated to Rev. and Hon. in business correspondence.

_____ 19. If a letter is addressed to a particular department in a company, the name of the department is placed on the first line and the name of the company on the second line.

_____ 20. A business title should not be hyphenated unless it represents a combination of two offices, such as secretary-treasurer.

ANSWERS TO QUIZ:

1. False Use a person's first name only if you know them as a friend.

2. False Companies or individuals who have a post office box are paying for that service and usually prefer to get their mail there. Many post offices deliver post office box mail more than once a day.

3. False As a rule of thumb, use the exact wording found on a company's letterhead when addressing letters to that company.

4. False This depends on how the company's name was registered. Thus if the registered name was NeXT Inc., no comma would be used.

5. False There is no limit to the length of the inside address, although you may want

to limit the length of a line as visually appropriate.

6. False This depends entirely on the length of the person's name and the length of his or her title. If both are short, they may be placed together on the same line and separated with a comma.

7. False Avoid abbreviations in all business correspondence whenever possible. Exceptions include Mr., Ms., Mrs., NE, SW, the dollar symbol ($) and zip code abbreviations.

8. False The salutation always agrees in number and gender with the top line of the inside address. If the top line is a company, the salutation needs to be plural, since companies are comprised of groups of people. Although we prefer not to use it, "Gentlemen" would be appropriate in this case.

9. False The date should be flush left, unless a modified block format is used, in which case it would be indented and aligned with the closing.

10. False Always use a person's name if you have it—try to get it if you don't.

11. False Don't make assumptions about an individual's gender—it's a sure way to alienate him or her if you guess wrong.

12. True This is an acceptable practice in today's business correspondence.

13. False Only spell out street names that are numbers if they are ten or below. For

higher numbers, use numerals. Also, use a company's letterhead for reference.

14. False   Avoid abbreviations in business letters whenever possible.

15. False   Letters addressed to someone's home are already assumed to be personal.

16. False   This usage, common in military correspondence, is not an accepted practice for business.

17. False   This would be redundant. Choose Dr. or Ph.D, but not both.

18. False   These titles are more formal and are therefore spelled out.

19. True   This is true if you do not have an individual's name for the first line of the inside address.

20. True   Vice President, when used as a title, is not hyphenated.

WHAT IF YOU DICTATE?

Dictation is a great help to some writers. It breaks writer's block, speeds up the writing process, and helps businesspeople write the way they speak. Dictation can tremendously increase your effectiveness and efficiency if you become skilled at it.

Even if you dictate, however, you still need to do some basic preparation in order to have a well-organized, carefully formatted sequence of thoughts, and not just a stream-of-consciousness rambling.

How can you avoid this problem? Simply by using the same planning stages that all good writers use. Analyze your audience and determine your purpose. All the same strategies and "prewriting" exercises that you undertake as a writer can be used when you dictate, allowing you to dictate with a plan. Move logically from one thought to the next.

Secretaries working from dictation equipment say that when the person dictating follows some type of keyword plan, the transcription job becomes much easier. And the final product emerges as much more powerful.

A secretary in a large construction company met with us and related her pet peeves about taking dictation. Her major complaint: "I would like, just once, to have each dictator listen to the jumble of incoherency I receive in a typical day."

Here is a list of dictating hints that each dictator should remember:

○ Make a game plan for the dictation. Most dictators jump from topic to topic with little noticeable relationship between each. A plan also makes rewrites much easier.

○ Use the pause (or stop) button when composing your thoughts. One dictator left the record button on for a full 15 minutes between paragraphs while he thought of what to say.

○ Turn the record button off when not dictating. When one dictator rode around town, he left the record button on. While he drove, he began talking to himself, swore, and blared the radio in the background. This made the secretary's job all the more difficult.

○ Be sure to spell out people's names, addresses, and all unfamiliar proper nouns.
Nothing infuriates a customer more than to
receive a letter with his or her name, address,
or other facts misspelled.

One broker reported that a major client called to respond to a proposal he had just received. After comment-
ing that the proposal was well-written and interesting, the
client added a "p.s.": "Hey Jim, next time I'd like my name
spelled properly." The worker looked embarrassed and
blushed as he told the story, and admitted that he was
lucky to have had such a congenial client.

Valuable contracts have been lost due to small errors in
business correspondence. Such mistakes are perceived as a
sign of sloppiness, which the customer thinks may carry
over to the execution of the contract.

Those are just a few pointers about dictation. Whether
you hand-write your first copy, dictate it, or type it on a
word processor, all modes work if you feel comfortable
using your particular style. Whichever method you use,
the underlying principles remain constant. And having a
plan to work from is the most important reminder of all.

Artists plan their paintings, potters sketch their products. As a creative, productive writer, you, too, now realize
the importance of careful planning techniques. Your
reader or supervisor will only see the results, so have fun
and be creative with the process. Let your mind drift into
areas of inspiration you never knew you had—free yourself up and let yourself enjoy this most important and
neglected phase of writing.

SOME BASIC RULES OF PUNCTUATION FOR BUSINESS WRITING

An interesting incident happened in one of our writing seminars. We were talking about punctuation — when and how to use it — and that the reality is that business writing todays demands fewer rather than more marks of punctuation. An alert woman raised her hand. In front of the group she confessed, "I like to use a lot of different marks of punctuation, just so my readers will think I'm more intelligent." She continued, "I'm not even certain that the marks I use are correct, but I figure that the more semicolons, question marks, colons, and exclamation points people find in my writing, the more intelligent they'll believe I am." We had to chuckle at her honesty. It's so typical of what people tend to do with all aspects of their writing!

The sad thing is, though, that instead of believing you to be smarter, your audiences will perceive you to be obscure, pretentious, and uninformed.

Punctuation is a vital and necessary part of good writing. In fact, the best writers know that they can have wonderful ideas and cleverly phrased sentences, but poor and inaccurate punctuation will ruin their writing.

THE POWER OF PROPER PUNCTUATION. Punctuation demands a book in itself. We recommend that in conjunction with a good grammar and reference text, you purchase a punctuation manual. Several are listed in Appendix C, Additional Resources for Business Writers. We will highlight here several aspects about punctuation that good business writers need to know.

PUT THE PERIOD.   The mark of punctuation most needed and least used in business writing is the period. Why? Because most writers create sentences that are much too long. They don't put the period soon enough. When do you put the period? When you have completed a thought. This mark of punctuation gives your reader a chance to pause, to digest what you've just written, and then to move smoothly to your next thought.

Instead of writing:

> *Poor:*   Your analysis of the brochure we published yesterday was coherent but I still would like some more concise explanations because many of your examples were vague.

> *Better:*   Your analysis of the brochure we published yesterday was coherent. But I still would like some more concise explanations. Many of your examples were vague.

CURBING COMMA FEVER.   The next vital mark of punctuation is the comma. English has dozens of rules for using the comma, and your grammar reference book will show them to you. Look at the sentence below and see how the writer has linked two independent or complete thoughts with a comma.

> *Poor:*   You should have received your check, we mailed it to you on February 20.

That's what editors call a "comma splice," or a run-on sentence. You should separate these two sentences by a period or semicolon, not a comma. Keep this rule in mind: commas can't separate sentences! Some of the other uses for commas are between items in a series, between lengthy introductory phrases and clauses, and between two clauses separated by conjunctions. You will come across these needs and uses as you are writing. Just keep in mind that the comma is an effective mark of punctuation for separating thoughts and phrases in your letter writing.

A lot of people have "comma fever"; that is, when they don't know what else to do with their punctuation, they insert a comma just to show any kind of pause or break. Although the comma is a necessary mark of punctuation, it can be overdone. You don't want to break up the flow of a sentence unnecessarily. Try just using commas where you would pause to take a breath when reading the sentence out loud. If you don't have a reason to use a comma, leave it out. The comma should not come too often in the flow of a sentence; otherwise, what you have is choppy rather than connected thoughts.

Avoid sentences like the following.

> *Poor:* Please, analyze, prepare, and evaluate, then, print out a new, complete brochure, so that James, the editor, can reread your work.

or

> *Poor:* That idea, which contradicts everyone else's, may be good, but it's a problem raiser, and we should, if we can, avoid problems, at all costs.

Delete commas and any other excesses. If you need to, begin new sentences where commas now exist. For example:

> *Better:* Please analyze, prepare, and evaluate. Then print out a new complete brochure so that James, our editor, can reread your work.

> *Better:* That idea contradicts everyone else's. It may be good, but it is a issue raiser. We should, if we can, avoid problems.

SECRETS FOR THE SEMICOLON. Now what about the semicolon? Many people are confused about when to use the semicolon; they don't really knowing what one is. A semicolon has two primary uses: (1) to separate independent clauses that are closely related or (2) to serve as a "supercomma" for a list of items when any one or more of those items contains a comma. Look at the sentence below and see how the writer has used the semicolon:

> *Good:* The original materials came from our
> Charleston plant; the finished product was made
> in Toledo.

That's one long sentence that could have been divided into two sentences with a period or separated by a comma and conjunction. But the two parts of the sentence are very closely connected and the semicolon shows the close link between them. Thus this semicolon separates independent clauses. Note that following the semicolon there is a complete thought. An alternative revision could read:

> *Good:* The original materials came from our
> Charleston plant, but the finished product was made
> in Toledo.

Both examples are grammatically correct. It is up to you to choose the style you want. By using both, you can add variety to your letters. Often when two sentences are closely related, the second part of the sentence following the semicolon begins with a transition or connective word such as "however."

> *Right:* We went to the store; however, they were all
> out of the items we needed.

The second use of a semicolon is as a supercomma. How many people are mentioned in the following sentence?

> *Wrong:* Jack, a junior, Jane, a senior, and Bill went
> to the movies.

The answer is unclear! You could have three named and two unnamed people or three people, two of whom happen to be a junior and a senior. To clarify this situation, a semicolon is needed.

> *Right:* Jack, a junior; Jane, a senior; and Bill went
> to the movies.

KNOWING ABOUT COLONS.   First cousin to the semicolon is the colon. Colons are primarily used to indicate that other material follows. The most effective use of the colon in business writing is to introduce a list or example.

> *Right:* The general manager called the meeting for
> two reasons:
>
> 1. To specifically identify the problem
>
> 2. To determine a feasible resolution to the problem

POSTURING THE APOSTROPHE. The apostrophe is a mark of punctuation used to show possession and contraction. First, possessives show ownership. "The manager's" shows ownership by the manager. That's not much of a problem. Most people get in trouble trying to decide where to put the apostrophe when the word ends in "s" or when they have a plural. Look at the following examples and see the correct uses of the apostrophe.

Singular	Singular Possessive	Plural	Plural Possessive
employer	employer's office	employers	employers' offices
week	week's work	weeks	two weeks' work
dollar	dollar's worth	dollar	5 dollars' worth
woman	woman's purse	women	women's purses

Rules for deciding where to put the apostrophe include:

1. Decide if the word showing possession is singular or plural.

2. If it is singular, add " 's."

3. If it is plural, and doesn't end in s, add " 's."

4. If it is plural, and ends in "s," add " ' " to the right of the "s."

Refer to a grammar book or comprehensive style guide for exceptions and more particular points regarding the possessive.

Apostrophes are also used for contractions. But, should you use contractions at all in business writing? Ten years ago most business letters, and reports avoided them. Words like "cannot, do not, should not" appeared instead of "can't," "don't," and "shouldn't." However, the trend in business today is toward more relaxed writing. There is nothing wrong with "can't," "don't" and "shouldn't" if they maintain rather than undermine the tone and purpose of your letter. The more formal the tone of the letter, the more contractions should be avoided.

If you use contractions in one part of your letter, try to be consistent and use them throughout. Look at the following sentence written by a well-intended business writer. Notice that what you see is a mixture of contractions and non-contracted forms.

> *Poor:* You *didn't* get your check because you *did not* send us the correct form. It *doesn't* matter when you return the form. *You are* entitled to your benefits.

If you mix and match contractions and the non-contracted form, you're shifting back and forth between the formal and the informal tone. That can create confusion and an inconsistent tone in your letter. Again, there is nothing wrong with using contractions if in fact your tone is informal, especially for in-house letters.

Your boss writes an informal letter:

> *Informal:* We can't meet tomorrow afternoon at 5 p.m. so we'll reschedule the meeting next Monday at lunch. I hope it's convenient for you.

The same letter could have been written:

> *Formal:* We cannot meet tomorrow at 5 p.m. so we will reschedule the meeting for next Monday at noon. I hope it is convenient for you.

The content is the same, but the tone is not. The second tone is more formal, distant, and perhaps does not make the reader feel as comfortable. After all, imagine that you are the listener. You want to be communicated with like a peer. Contractions can sometimes relax your words enough so that even bad news can be softened.

HYPHENS.   Hyphens cause most writers a lot of confusion. You should hyphenate compound adjectives when they are used together *before* the noun they modify:

> *Right:* The well-known engineer.

But not if they *follow* the noun:

>*Right:* The engineer was well known.

Be especially careful with numbers.

>*Right:* He painted three 40-foot ceilings.

>*Right:* The neighborhood had two-, three-, and four-bedroom houses.

Adverbs, which typically end in "ly," are not hyphenated.

>*Right:* The highly recommended report finally arrived.

USING DASHES AND PARENTHESES.   Many people are unclear of the meaning and use of dashes (represented on a typewriter by two adjacent hyphens) and parentheses. Use dashes to indicate a break in thought, or to highlight and give greater importance to additional information inserted in a sentence. Use parentheses to diminish tangential information that is added. If the inserted information is about as important as the information in the sentence itself, set it apart with commas.

>*Right:* Mary, feeling low, decided not to come to the party.

>*Right:* Mary—who was having the worst day of her life—skipped the party.

>*Right:* Mary (she parked the car crooked) decided not to go to the party.

A dash can also be used to set off information at the end of a sentence.

> *Right:* We all signed the contract—finally.

Parentheses are also used if you give a lengthy name of a company or document, and then give the abbreviated form or acronym, for example, Employee Assistance Program (EAP). The parentheses should enclose the acronym when it first appears. You can then refer to the acronym only, without parentheses, throughout the rest of the letter. This is one way you can use abbreviations in your letter and be certain your reader knows their meaning—even then, however, don't overuse acronyms.

QUOTING QUOTATION MARKS.   Quotation marks are necessary and functional marks of punctuation. Most people know that quotation marks are effective in indicating what someone has said. The problem is not when but how to use them. Below are examples of the proper uses for quotation marks.

1. Rule 1. Periods and commas always go inside quotation marks.

    He said, "Let's meet soon."

2. Rule 2. Semicolons and colons always go outside quotation marks.

    He said, "Let's meet soon"; however, no meeting was scheduled.

3. Rule 3. Exclamation points and question
          marks go inside or outside the quota-
          tion marks depending on the sense of
          the sentence.

Have you read "Business News"?

We are going to discuss the question

"What is our strategy on the Miller Project?"

He shouted "Watch out!"

Watch out for "bozos"!

Again, a complete grammar reference book will give you sound guidelines for using quotation marks, but those three rules should help.

Many business writers are hesitant to use the question mark and the exclamation point. I recommend that if you are trying to achieve variety in vocabulary, style, and format, that you experiment and use both interrogative and exclamatory sentences, where appropriate.

What's wrong with starting a letter with a question? It's a very effective way of drawing your reader into your letter and getting him or her involved in the subject matter. Have you ever attended a speech where the speaker opens with a question? Immediately, the audience looks up. They are involved. They're drawn into the subject. You can do the same by opening a letter with a question, speaking directly to your reader, rather than speaking at him or her. "What are your thoughts on the Simington project?" "Can you arrange a meeting in my office at 5 p.m. tomorrow afternoon?" Those are effective letter openers that directly address the topic and attract your readers' attention.

To express emotion, there's nothing wrong with writing, "That was a great report you gave yesterday afternoon!"

Unconventional punctuation, like offbeat vocabulary, can be overdone, overused, and inappropriate. But a modest sprinkling of various punctuation marks, used appropriately, energizes your writing. Punctuation need not be a terribly complex subject, and you certainly don't have to review your seventh grade English notes in order to learn it. However, knowing and using the correct punctuation will increase your confidence in your writing. See Appendix A, A Compendium of English Usage, for a more extensive guide to grammar, punctuation, and word usage.

PART TWO

WRITE IT

CHAPTER 6

BASIC RULES OF GOOD BUSINESS WRITING

WRITE THE WAY YOU SPEAK

GET TO THE POINT

BE CLEAR AND CONCISE

BE POSITIVE

Once you've decided on your content, the following rules can help you to say it best. These rules apply not only to letters, but also to memos, proposals, reports, and any other writing you may do. These rules will greatly improve your writing, and they are simple, besides! The four keys we advocate to turn your sentences into direct, dynamic statements with powerful, purposeful messages are: (1) write the way you speak, (2) get to the point, (3) be clear and concise, and (4) be positive. These rules are painless, and you can easily implement them in your own writing.

WRITE THE WAY YOU SPEAK

The simplest rule we advocate — and one of the most important — is to write the way you speak. This will make it easier for you to begin writing and create a good first draft.

Many writers focus too much on how they're going to write and not enough on how their writing will sound. Don't overlook your "ear." As your first step, ask yourself, "How would I say this to the person I'm writing to if he or she were sitting across from me?" Worry about the polish later on. The best letters almost write themselves. The ideas, their flow, the specific word choice and phrasing — these should all be in the natural communication patterns of the person writing. Once you have that first draft, you can then remove the communication "blemishes" or verbal faults that occur when you speak!

Imagine your staff sitting around a table. You must write them a letter about a forthcoming meeting. What would you *say* to them if they were there with you right now? Does it "ring" right? A well-tuned sentence is not the one with complicated vocabulary and poetic lyrics. (Save those passages for your personal letters or your next novel!) The best business writing sounds like the best business conversation: brief, clear, direct, relaxed.

By their very design and purpose, most letters are short. All you have to do is to imagine a brief conversation and put your ideas in writing.

Good conversationalists know that the best conversations occur when they're in tune with their audiences, be it one or one hundred people. But how do they do this? Simple. They focus on their listeners. They ask, "Who's going to read this? What does that person already know about the topic? What do they need to know to take the action requested in the letter?"

Working from your plan for your letter, that is, the outline for what you want to cover and in what order, fill out your thoughts on paper. Depending upon how much planning you did, this step will be easy. If, for example, you used freewriting as one of your prewriting steps, you will have a comprehensive listing of all your thoughts on the topic and can more readily shape and condense those thoughts in the refining stage. In other words, the more you do in the planning stage, the easier it is to write!

Business correspondence uses the language of polite, professional people, so avoid slang, cliches, and off-color remarks when you draft your correspondence. Otherwise, you will need to edit out these inappropriate expressions.

Most people experience some difficulty in actually starting to write. The reasons why vary from person to person. Many writers struggle because they feel they have to turn out perfect copy the first time. Others report being embarrassed by poor spelling skills.

Most people compose with two voices simultaneously competing inside of them. One's the writer: creative and uncensored; the other's the editor: critical, judgmental, repressive. The problem is that the editor comes into play too early in most people's writing process. This "bad guy" kills off too many good ideas before they ever get on paper. That's not to say that the editorial voice isn't necessary; to the contrary, it's a vital voice. But it appears much later in the process, not in the beginning.

During the first stages of writing, when you're deciding on ideas to insert, be lenient. Now's the relaxed time when no one's looking — not your boss, your colleagues, or your worst critic! You'll discover during these first planning stages that you're much more creative than you ever have given yourself credit for.

GET TO THE POINT

Many business writers are long-winded when they start to write. They may rehash a previous letter or drone on about background information that the reader already knows. Many writers are guilty of not taking adequate time to think about what they want to say (and *why* they want to say it) before they start to write. Instead they use the beginning of a letter to "warm up" to the topic; they write *about* the topic of the letter without actually making the relevant points the reader needs at this time.

When asked about advice to aspiring novelists, Kurt Vonnegut, Jr. suggested: "Throw away your first seven pages!" He went on to describe that good writing starts as close to the action as possible and that most writers feel compelled to have a laborious introduction to their story that is more often than not boring to readers.

This advice is all the more valid for business writing. (Because of the length of business letters, we opt for throwing out only the first paragraph!) Your readers will appreciate the respect you have for their time in getting right to the point. Your letters will be fresher — uncluttered with unimportant information — and you will appear to be more decisive.

If you ask yourself only one question before you write a business letter, let it be "What do I most want to say to this person on this topic?" and let the answer be the starting point for your letter.

BE CLEAR AND CONCISE

Once you start the letter off by getting directly to the point, continue by being clear and concise throughout the entire letter. Many people tend to overwrite, and produce long, rambling responses. One reason people write more than they might speak is that they have more time to consider their answers, and are therefore able to explain in fuller detail. Perhaps they are afraid of leaving out some details. Every time they read over the letter they add a few more points to further "clarify" what they mean.

Unfortunately, far from clarifying the message, such excessive writing often muddles what you have to say. It often is full of redundancies, tangential thoughts and expressions, and cliches. The recipient is often forced to reread the letter, hunting for the main points. You have placed the burden of understanding the communication unfairly upon your reader.

We have found that lack of clarity is the most commonly reported problem concerning most business writing. Readers too often do not understand what is being stated, why it is being stated, the consequences to the reader, and the actions the reader should take as a result. In other words, unclear writing is practically worthless.

Make your points, make them clearly, make them once, and stop.

One of the advantages of writing is that you can deliberately form powerful sentences that say exactly what you want in exactly the way you want. If you haven't made things clear in your first draft, you have the option of revising your writing again and again until it serves your purposes. In fact, a major part of good writing is actually the ability to effectively edit!

There are only two exceptions for not being as concise as possible in all your business writing. The first exception, as discussed earlier (and in more detail in Chapter 9), is when you have negative news to relate. In such instances you should first "buffer" your message with a reason or positive statement to help soften the message. The second exception, to be discussed next, is when the words you are adding help to improve the "goodwill" or positive feel of the letter.

BE POSITIVE

All professional business writing sould be positive. Or, if negative information is communicated, do so in as positive a manner as possible. Positive letters emphasize good news, are complimentary in a sincere way, and whenever possible suggest acceptable alternatives rather than make demands. Why is this? First, since business letters are sent to individuals outside of the company, there is a public relations aspect to every communication.

Regardless of the letter's message, you should try to somehow leave the reader thinking more highly of your company. If you are positive and courteous, readers will more likely feel they have been treated fairly and professionally—even if they are given bad news—than if your correspondence is curt and negative. Even if you have to deny a customer request, turn down a job applicant, or be critical of a supplier, you need to consistently do so in positive ways. The effect of your business correspondence compounded by the hundreds or thousands of letters your company sends each day helps to create a positive company image that can indirectly translate into increased business, satisfied customers, and happy employees.

We'll discuss more about being positive when we talk about tone in Chapter 8.

CHAPTER 7

BUILDING BLOCKS TO BETTER WRITING

WORD CHOICE

PHRASES

SENTENCES

PARAGRAPHS

Now that we've gone over some basic guidelines that can significantly improve your business writing, we'd like to discuss the specific elements that comprise your business letters: words, phrases, sentences, and paragraphs.

WORD CHOICE

The basis of all good writing is effective word selection. "The right word," said Mark Twain, "is the difference between 'lightning' and a 'lightning bug.'" If your writing is not founded on clear, simple words, it will be more difficult to read and comprehend.

USE SHORT, CONVERSATIONAL WORDS

Use short, spoken transitions over long, bookish ones. By using short words, you help set an ordinary, informal tone for the rest of what you say. Since conversational, everyday words communicate best, also avoid the use of *jargon*, the technical language of a specific group. Jargon should be avoided in business writing unless you are certain that your reader will understand the terms you use.

USE CONVERSATIONAL WORDS

More Formal	More Relaxed
consequently	so
however	but
in addition	also
nevertheless	still

BE SIMPLE AND SPECIFIC

Whenever you have a choice, select the word that best fits what you mean. But do not spend excessive time trying to hunt for the exact word in a dictionary or thesaurus. Chances are if you have to consult a dictionary to find the exact word you want, the reader will have to consult a dictionary to see what that word means! The end result is that it looks as if you are trying to impress your reader rather than clearly communicate your thoughts.

This is not to say that an extensive vocabulary is not important—it is. But your language should not be "forced." Given reflective time, you are apt to find the right word in your everyday vocabulary.

EFFECTIVE WORD SELECTION

concrete (car)	rather than	abstract (transportation)
simple (use)	rather than	complex (utilize)
specific (tomorrow)	rather than	general (soon)
positive (solutions)	rather than	negative (problems)
appropriate (call)	rather than	slang (phone)

AVOID MISUSED AND OVERUSED WORDS

Be on the lookout for commonly misused words in business writing (the most common of these are presented in Appendix A). For example, many business people are guilty of creating verbs such as "ok'ed" (as in "My manager ok'ed this request"). Other words, such as "anxious" to mean "eager" (instead of nervous) and "candidate" to refer to things (instead of people) are simply incorrect. Though your reader may understand your meaning, such word misuse is still incorrect and sloppy.

Overused words also present problems for the business writer. Any word can lose its meaning and effectiveness if used to excess. If you overuse groups of words, the credibility of your writing will suffer. For example, the overuse of adjectives, which modify or enhance nouns, has been widely practiced in advertising and thus has seemingly become acceptable in modern life. It is not enough that a new detergent simply be described as "new"; today it seems as if the product may be inferior if it is not described as "super, new and improved, with special cleansing action" in order to attract our attention. The effectiveness of our language suffers as a result.

This same problem creeps into business writing when we attempt to modify a word when its meaning is already clear. For example, a "knowledgeable expert" is meaningless if you consider the fact that an "expert" is already someone who is very knowledgeable. Likewise, the "absolute maximum" is redundant since "maximum" already means the most possible, and the "very" in "very unique" is unnecessary since "unique" already means "one of a kind." Avoid such unnecessary and potentially confusing uses of words when you write.

```
WATCH YOUR USE OF INTENSIFIERS

    exceedingly        positively
    extremely          quite
    greatly            really
    highly             truly
    indeed             very
    most               wonderful
```

```
AVOID UNQUALIFIABLES
Unqualifiable              Preferred

absolute maximum          maximum
absolute minimum          minimum
complete monopoly         monopoly
entirely completed        completed
absolutely essential      essential
most unique               unique
most correct              correct
most exact                exact
qualified expert          expert
```

USE SIMPLE VERBS

The most important words you use in writing are your verbs—the action words of your sentences. Writing that uses clear, simple, active verbs is energetic and powerful.

Some people enter our writing seminars with painful memories of their junior high school grammar classes. Our primary grammar lesson is learning the value of the verb. Verbs create power in your writing. The central word in your sentence is the verb. It's the action word, the only one that can actually do something for you. Most people rely on weak or inactive verbs rather than strong and active verbs. Their sentences sit rather than move on the page. That's exactly the opposite of what you want to accomplish.

Verbs involve either "action" or "being." Good business writing minimizes the use of "being" verbs such as "is," "are," "was," "will be," "can," or "should" because they are so inactive.

VERBS GIVE WRITING ENERGY!

Use verbs that are:

simple	direct
short	active

MINIMIZE USE OF "BEING" VERBS

am	had
are	has
be	have
became	is
been	was
being	will
could	would

Use action verbs instead!

USE "ACTIVE" VERBS

Action verbs move your sentence along; they communicate movement, power, and direction. Whenever you can, turn a being verb into an action verb, and you will enhance your sentence tremendously. For example, in the sentence

> *Fair:* He is a strong writer.

the "active" verb is hidden in another part of speech, in this case the noun "writer." We call this finding the "smothered verb." To improve this sentence, turn the noun into your verb, and you will have a more powerful and effective sentence:

> *Better:* He writes strongly.

or

> *Better:* He writes effectively.

Here is another example.

> *Fair:* My new assistant is negligent in her work.

Look at the verb "is." It does nothing to enhance the sentence. The key to the statement is the word "negligent," or maybe "work." If you scan that sentence with our verbal geiger counter, you pick up both of those. Rewrite it.

> *Better:* My new assistant neglects some of her work.

or

> *Better:* My new assistant works irresponsibly (or irregularly, inconsistently . . .).

Some other frequently used verbs are weak rather than strong. Stay away from using "do, make, seem, appear, be," and "get." All are grammatically correct, but they lack power. Whenever possible, replace them with more active verbs. Look at this sentence:

> *Poor:* This directive is applicable to all personnel who make use of our system.

Our weak verbs show up again: "is" and "make." You can easily tighten up this sentence by writing,

> *Better:* This directive applies to all personnel who use our system.

These simple changes create meaning, power, and impact in the entire sentence. Certain nouns frequently smother active verbs. "Authorization" is one of them. It's also a popular word in the business world.

> *Poor:* The authorization for the trip was given by my supervisor.

> *Better:* My supervisor authorized the trip.

You may notice that words ending in "ion" such as authorization, production, hesitation, and completion, often smother verbs. Shifting away from such endings is not difficult and will result in more readable business writing.

AVOID NOUN ENDINGS ON VERBS

clarify	not	clarification
dependent	not	dependence
stagnant	not	stagnated
adjust	not	adjustable
maintains	not	maintaining of
establishing	not	establishment

ACTION VERBS

act	classify	deliver
activate	coach	demonstrate
adapt	collect	design
address	communicate	detail
adopt	compile	detect
advertise	complete	determine
advise	compose	develop
analyze	compute	devise
anticipate	conduct	diagnose
apply	confront	direct
appraise	conserve	discover
arrange	consolidate	dispense
assemble	construct	display
assess	consult	disprove
assist	contract	dissect
attain	control	distribute
audit	coordinate	divert
budget	correspond	draft
build	counsel	dramatize
calculate	create	edit
catalog	defer	educate
change	define	electrify
chart	delegate	eliminate

ACTION VERBS (cont.)

enforce	inspire	perfect
enlarge	install	perform
entertain	institute	persuade
estimate	instruct	photograph
evaluate	integrate	pilot
examine	interpret	pioneer
exhibit	interview	plan
expand	introduce	play
explain	invent	predict
express	inventory	prepare
extract	investigate	prescribe
familiarize	judge	preserve
figure	lead	preside
file	lecture	print
filter	maintain	process
fix	manage	produce
formulate	map	program
forward	market	project
gather	measure	promote
govern	mediate	propose
guide	model	protect
head	modify	provide
help	monitor	publicize
hire	motivate	purchase
identify	navigate	quote
illustrate	negotiate	raise
improve	observe	reason
index	obtain	recommend
indoctrinate	operate	reconcile
influence	order	record
inform	organize	recruit
initiate	originate	reduce
innovate	paint	refer
inspect	participate	rehabilitate

render
reorganize
repair
replace
report
represent
research
resolve
respond
restore
retrieve
review
revise
save
schedule
select
shape

simplify
sketch
solve
sort
spark
specify
stimulate
straighten
streamline
strengthen
study
suggest
summarize
supervise
supply
survey
synthesize

systematize
tabulate
talk
test
time
train
transcribe
transfer
translate
transmit
treat
tutor
unify
upgrade
vitalize
write

ACTIVE VOICE

Changing the verb in your sentences from the passive to the active voice strengthens phrases and sentences. This is a subtle shift. Here's how it works: when trying to understand the difference between passive and active voice, think in terms of the types of people you know. A passive person lets things happen to him or her. An active person makes things happen. The same is true in business writing. Passive voice verbs delay the action; they focus on receiving action rather than accomplishing or creating action. They also pose word order problems.

Poor: The plant was inspected by the supervisor.

Who's supposed to be the actor in that sentence? The supervisor, yet that person receives the action. All you have to do to change your sentence from passive to active is ask yourself, "Who is doing what to whom?" In the sentence above, the supervisor is doing the action to the plant, so switch the word order around.

> *Better:* The supervisor inspected the plant.

This revision does three very important things. First, it shifts the sentence from passive to active; you have the doer accomplish rather than receive the action. Second, you eliminate the weak "being" verb and substitute an active, strong verb, "inspected." Third, you tighten and shorten your sentence.

You win all the way around when you move from the passive to the active in your business letters. A verb in the passive voice combines any form of the verb "to be" with the past participle of the main verb; that is, the passive uses "am," "is," "are," "was," "were," "be," "being," "been," plus a main verb that usually ends in "en" or "ed." Who are the actors in the next sentence?

> *Poor:* Appropriate clothing will be worn by all personnel.

Just move the actors to the beginning of the sentence, and it will now read,

> *Better:* All personnel will wear appropriate clothing.

Or, if you want to give a directive,

> *Better:* Wear appropriate clothing.

(You can always soften your directive with "please".)

The latter sentences are tighter, cleaner, and certainly more direct and effective. Another example:

> *Poor:* He was regarded poorly by his supervisor.

An improvement:

> *Better:* His supervisors regarded him poorly.

This brings up an interesting point. Numerous people hide behind the passive and duck responsibility for something that they feel, decide, or do. Many performance evaluations employ passive-voice verbs, especially when there is bad news.

Another way to know if you're writing in the passive voice is if you use the preposition "by" and follow it with what should be the subject of your sentence. Here's an example:

> *Poor:* The card was issued by The Price Club.

Instead write:

> *Better:* The Price Club issued the card.

In a passive sentence the verb often directly precedes the word "by."

ACTIVE WRITING

Using active verbs and the active voice constitutes what is known as active writing. Good business writing is almost always written actively since active writing provides energy, clarity, and directness to your message.

When you write actively your writing will tend to have more personality as well. Active writing helps eliminate stiff, inactive verbs and overused phrases. It encourages you to communicate in your own style, and not a forced, pompous one. As a result, the way you write will be a reflection of the way you speak, which will parallel the way you think—which is the essence of who you are!

Occasionally, you may still want to write in a passive style in some of your business correspondence, such as (1) when you want to be especially formal ("An announcement has been made . . ."), (2) when you want to obscure responsibility ("An error has been found . . ."), or (3) when you want to buffer negative messages ("Your suggestion has been considered . . .").

The key is having the skill to write actively or passively, so that you can choose to write whichever way is appropriate.

PHRASES

In the simplest form, words are combined into phrases as a way of forming thoughts. Phrases, too, should come naturally from the way you speak. They tend to be best when they are simple, direct, and easy to visualize.

Business writers tend to overuse certain phrases. When this happens, a phrase loses its freshness and meaning, and thus clutters up what might otherwise be effective communication. Some examples of overused phrases are:

At the beginning of letters:

○ The purpose of this letter is . . .

○ Regarding your recent letter . . .

○ Per our conversation . . .

○ Pursuant to . . .

At the closing of letters:

○ Please find enclosed . . .

○ Please advise as to the status of . . .

○ Feel free to contact me . . .

○ Hoping to hear from you soon . . .

○ May I expect your response soon?

○ Please don't hesitate to call . . .

○ Thanking you in advance . . .

These overused phrases are so common that readers must often look beyond the letter opening to find the new message being communicated.

In addition, good writing avoids calling attention to the communication itself, a fault found in the following phrases:

○ As already stated . . .

○ It has long been known that . . .

○ As you probably already know . . .

If the reader already knows, then why are you saying it?

- ○ I wish to state that . . .
- ○ It may be said . . .
- ○ It is interesting to note . . .

Just say it!

USE PHRASES THAT ARE:

- ○ Simple and direct
- ○ Literal and easy to visualize

MAKE PHRASES ACTIVE!

Passive	*Active* (possible improvement)
be it known that	(eliminate this phrase)
decentralization was necessitated	we decentralized
by evidence which presented itself	because of evidence we received
via certain surveys which	from surveys that
during an earlier stage	we initially thought
had been initially deemed inappropriate	was not needed
to the designing of	to design
the organizational structure	the organization

SENTENCES

Once you have a basis for forming clear phrases, you are able to effectively write complete thoughts, otherwise known as sentences. Every sentence should have an actor (subject) and an action (verb). Sentences are clearest when they communicate a single idea or thought in a simple, direct format (such as a subject/verb format). When your writing becomes difficult to understand, just simplify what you are saying and the order in which you are saying it to clarify your sentences.

PREFER SHORTER SENTENCES

Sentence length can vary, ranging from shorter sentences (for emphasis) to longer sentences (to communicate more complex thoughts). Most business writers today, however, tend to write sentences that are consistently too long. This is a result of excessive add-on information connected by "ands" or weakly connected by commas. Fight this tendency in your own writing by using shorter, more direct sentences. Get in the habit of stopping sentences at the end of each complete thought.

Are you thinking that it might be difficult to let go of lengthy phrases, passive verbs, and long words, because you won't sound intelligent? If that's your initial reaction, you're not alone.

But our nation is changing its habits. A large southwestern bank gives its top executives only half sheets to write on. They know that when given a full sheet, most of us will fill it up. They don't want top management to spend too much time on their writing, and the half sheets limit the tendency to use long and wordy sentences.

Why not bring some of these changes into your own company?

SENTENCES

○ Communicate single ideas or thoughts

○ Vary in length

  Shorter for emphasis

  Longer for complex ideas

○ Are clearest in a simple, direct format

  WATCH FOR run-on sentences created by excessive use of "and" or commas

---

COMMON SENTENCE MISTAKES

Let's take a look at some of the most frequent sentence errors made in business writing.

VERB/SUBJECT AGREEMENT. The verb of a sentence needs to agree in number (singular or plural) with the subject.

> *Right:* There are two parts to this program.

> *Right:* Mr. Olsen and his two assistants *were* working on the program.

> *Right:* Mr. Olsen, as well as his two assistants, *was* working on the program.

The subject of a sentence is never the object of a prepositional phrase.

> *Wrong:* Each of the players *were* told to run laps after practice.

"Each," which is always singular, is the subject, so the correct verb is "was." Some people might be fooled by the plural "players," which is closer to the verb. But look closely: "players" is part of a prepositional phrase ("of the players").

> *Right:* Each of the players *was* told to run laps after practice.

In either/or sentence constructions, the verb agrees with the closer subject.

> *Wrong:* Either the contractor or the draftsmen *was* at fault.

> *Right:* Either the contractor or the draftsmen *were* at fault" or "Either the draftsmen or the contractor *was* at fault.

Some words (team, jury, committee, choir) can be singular or plural depending upon how they are used, and their implied meaning in the sentence.

> *Right:* The jury is going to announce *its* verdict today.

> *Right:* The jury will go home after announcing *their* verdict today."

> *Better:* Members of the jury are going to go home
> after *their* verdict is announced.

MODIFICATION/CLARITY.
Sentence modifiers should be placed as close to what is being modified in the sentence as possible for clarity.

> *Wrong:* I have been trying to place him under con-
> tract to work here for three years.

Has the speaker been trying for three years, or are we talking about a three-year contract? Clarifying the meaning is the responsibility of the writer!

> *Right:* For three years I have been trying to place
> him under contract to work here.

> *Wrong:* We found a pile of photos in the corner,
> which had not been dusted for three years.

What had not been dusted? The photos or the corner?

> *Right:* In the corner we found a pile of photos, which
> had not been dusted for three years.

> *Wrong:* A blender may crack when boiling water is
> poured in unless it is running.

> *Right:* Unless it is running, a blender may crack
> when boiling water is poured in.

> *Wrong:* Having finished the job, the drop cloths were
> removed.

This sentence has no actor—the drop cloths could not have finished the job!

Right: Having finished the job, the painters removed the drop cloths.

Many ambiguous references are caused by sloppy or excessive use of pronouns (words that rename nouns, that is, people, places, or things). A typical letter that has this fault may mention several different people, then in a new sentence refer to "he." The reference is then unclear; which person is being referred to?

Wrong: He refused to have him call her on Monday.

Wrong: His manager asked him regularly to call him.

To avoid confusion with pronouns in your sentences, simply use nouns or proper nouns instead of pronouns.

PARALLEL STRUCTURE.   Good business writing has parallel structure; that is, there is similar treatment in the structure of sentences, lists, letters, etc.

Wrong: We hope the treaty will provide peace, a harmony, and fair conditions for both sides.

Right: We hope the treaty will provide peace, harmony, and fairness for both sides.

Here is another sample sentence written in parallel form:

Right: The purpose of the workshop was to discuss state, local, and federal water quality regulations, to debate the economic impact of waste control, and to devise concepts and methods of monitoring wastes.

Those items as listed are all in parallel form; they are items in a series, all approximately the same length, and all introduced by the infinitive ("to discuss . . . to debate . . . to devise).

When lists are numbered or lettered, they should also be presented in parallel form. A bank employee composed the next list.

> *Poor:* The status information immediately informs us of: (a) Is it a statement or is it a passbook? (b) is account open or is it closed? (c) effective date of account opened? (d) prior transaction (e) statement cycle (f) interest pay cycle.

The writer has itemized the status information. But the list is not in parallel form. The problem with this list is that the writer starts out with two questions: "Is it a statement or a passbook?" and "is the account open or closed?" and then shifts to a series of statements rather than questions. Also, each list entry should complete the sentence introduced by the phrase preceding the colon.

To make this list parallel, you can turn those final three items to questions, and revise the opening phrase.

> The status information answers the following questions: (a) Is it a statement or a passbook? (b) Is it open or closed? (c) What was the effective date the account was opened? (d) What was the account balance? (e) What was the interest date? (f) What was the interest pay cycle?

PLACE LISTS IN PARALLEL FORM

○ Keep listed items brief

○ Begin with verbs when possible

○ Use the same verb tenses

○ Limit sublists

○ Prefer three to five points

PARAGRAPHS

Now put your sentences together into powerful paragraphs! Again, writing a good paragraph is not difficult if you follow a few easy guidelines. Each of your paragraphs should center around its own theme, often stated in the first sentence of the paragraph. For example, in a letter of inquiry, the first paragraph would be about your request, the second paragraph might be a justification of the request, and the third paragraph might be a "thank you" for the requested item. Your paragraph structure should reflect the organized flow of your thoughts.

VARY YOUR PARAGRAPH LENGTH

Paragraphs should vary in length: shorter for emphasis or ease in reading, longer to explain more complex or detailed topics. Letters which have too many short paragraphs comes across as choppy. Letters with only long and detailed paragraphs usually have little direction and are unappealing to the reader. If you follow the guidelines discussed so far, especially those regarding sentence construction, you won't need to worry about having paragraphs that drag on.

Shorter paragraphs eliminate the monotony of solid blocks of type on a page. Don't be hampered by the traditional literary definition of a paragraph as a group of related sentences forming a unit of thought. This would encourage you to write letters which were one long paragraph, since the best business letters focus on one idea only. Use brief paragraphs as a device to make the letter easier to read.

Look at the following two examples of a letter:

> Dear Ms. Reynolds:
>
> We are pleased that you will be attending the Manager's Day on Monday, March 3. The program will be held at the Los Rios Marriott, 3344 Los Rios Drive (just north of the city); a map is enclosed for your convenience. The program will begin promptly at 2:00 p.m. and will end at 6:00 p.m., followed by a wine and cheese reception. If you would like overnight accommodations, a block of rooms has been reserved at the Los Rios Marriott at a special rate. To make arrangements, please call Mary Miller at our Los Rios office, (619) 999-9999.
>
> Please call if you need more information. We look forward to seeing you on March 3.
>
> Sincerely,
>
>
> Patty Petals

This letter contains important information for the reader, but who wants to spend time wading through the first paragraph? It is much more inviting when it is broken up this way:

Dear Ms. Reynolds:

We are pleased that you plan to attend Manager's Day on Monday, March 3.

The program will be held at the Los Rios Marriott, 3344 Los Rios Drive, just north of the city. We've enclosed a map for your convenience.

We will begin the program promptly at 2:00 p.m. and will end at 6:00 p.m. A wine and cheese reception will follow.

If you would like overnight accommodations, we've reserved a block of rooms at the Los Rios Marriott at a special rate. To make arrangements, call Mary Miller at our Los Rios office, (619) 999-9999.

Please call if you need more information. We look forward to seeing you on March 3.

Sincerely,

Patty Petals

The paragraphs are brief, clear, and ample white space appears on the page to lure the reader into the text.

ORGANIZE YOUR PARAGRAPHS CAREFULLY

You've grabbed the reader's attention with a direct and interesting opening paragraph. Now, be certain that the remainder of the letter keeps the level of reader interest high.

Complete your letter by including all the information you wish to cover in the most organized manner possible. It's a good idea to make a list of the points you wish to address and then work those into your letter as you write.

As with memos, it's important not to cover too many ideas in one letter. The points should all relate to one single topic. If you cover too much you not only confuse the reader, you also make it difficult for him or her to respond.

PARAGRAPHS

○ Communicate thoughts related to a common theme

○ Help with organization and flow of ideas

○ Vary in length averaging 4 to 5 sentences

Shorter for emphasis or ease in reading

Longer for heavy detail

○ Are clearest when they have a topic sentence and clear references

---

USE TRANSITIONS TO CONNECT YOUR THOUGHTS

As you read from paragraph to paragraph, make sure that your organization is clear, and that your writing flows. You can accomplish this flow by using effective openings, clear topic sentences; and smooth transitions. Transitions are words like "however," "moreover," "nevertheless," and "therefore," or the more relaxed "but," "and," "so," and "first."

The following list gives some examples of transitions that can be used to:

Show cause and effect: accordingly, as a result, hence, therefore

Show exceptions to what has been said: but, even though, on the contrary, otherwise, conversely, however, on the other hand

Indicate time, place or order in relation to what has gone before: above all, finally, in summary, still, after all, first, meanwhile, then, again, further, next, too

Introduce examples: for example, for instance, namely, that is

Other transitional or connective words that you can use to link your sentences include the following:

Addition: moreover, further, furthermore, besides, and, and then, likewise, also, nor, too, again, in addition, equally important, next, first, second, third (etc.), finally, last,

Contrast: but, yet, and yet, however, still, nevertheless, on the other hand, on the contrary, after all, notwithstanding, for all that, in contrast to this, at the same time, although this may be true, otherwise.

Comparison: similarly, likewise, in like manner.

Purpose: to this end, for this purpose, with this object.

Result: hence, therefore, accordingly, consequently, thus, thereupon, wherefore, as a result.

Time: meanwhile, at length, immediately, soon, after a few days, in the meantime, afterward, later

Place: hereby, beyond, nearby, opposite to, adjacent to, on the opposite side

Summary, repetition, exemplification, intensification: to sum up, in brief, on the whole, in sum, in short, as I have said, in other words, to be sure, as has been noted, for example, for instance, in fact, indeed, in any event

Regardless of the style of transitions you choose, we recommend that you have a modest, yet definite, sprinkling of transitions from paragraph to paragraph, idea to idea. This helps your reader move easily and smoothly from one idea to the next. After all, you want to be understood. As with any tool, however, you don't want to overdo it with transitions. One per paragraph is usually enough.

Another way to move smoothly between paragraphs is to take a word from the last sentence of one paragraph and use it in the first sentence of the next paragraph. Here's an example:

> . . . you should attract many viewers with these excellent *locations*.

> Many people have reserved these *locations* to exhibit . . .

In addition, try using a sentence to make a transition between paragraphs. For example:

> Reports show that people take road trips based on the price of gasoline. Some organizations, like hotels, want to keep the price of gas down to increase traveling — and business.

> *But authorities prove that the price of gas doesn't necessarily reflect the number of road trips people take.*

They showed that although the price of gas went
down in some cases, hotel reservations stayed the
same or even increased. Apparently, other factors
influence road trips—the cost of foreign travel,
weather conditions, and the prices of other necessi-
ties such as clothing and food.

Another way to make a transition is to use headers to
announce the contents of the paragraph that follows.
Here's an example:

PAY DAY

Pay day will be on Monday. The 15th falls on the
weekend this month.

CHAPTER 8

Style and Tone

WHAT IS WRITING STYLE?

HOW DOES TONE DIFFER FROM STYLE?

WORDS THAT CREATE EMOTIONAL RESPONSES

So far we have mainly discussed the mechanical aspects of writing. Two final elements that are important to quality writing are less tangible: style and tone.

WHAT IS WRITING STYLE?

The way you combine your words and sentences to convey your thoughts determines the style of your writing. Style is the background music to your writing. Your style can be stiff and formal, warm and soothing, clipped, monotonous, or as many other varieties as there are people.

Your style plays a role in how your business letters will be received by your readers. If your choice and arrangement of words seem condescending and sarcastic, for example, you are less likely to get your reader to react favorably to any request you might have. If, on the other hand, you seem professional, sincere, and courteous, the reader's reaction is more likely to be favorable to you, your message, and any action you are suggesting he or she take.

It is difficult to teach style because it does not lend itself to specific rules or formulas for writing. It is almost easier to describe what not to do to develop your own style rather than what to do. For example, one of the classic books on writing and grammar, *The Elements of Style* (William Strunk, Jr. and E. B. White, New York: Macmillan, 3rd ed. 1979), suggests that you will develop your style if you "write in a way that comes naturally to you." Yet how one does this is more a function of what you do not do—namely, by not using stodgy or contrived or technical language, passive and deadened verbs, or overused expressions and cliches.

If you follow the guidelines for writing described earlier in this book, all that remains is your own way of saying things—hence, your own style of communicating will emerge!

We advocate that your style of writing for business be conversational and simple so as to be as easy to understand as possible. In this way your style will not get in the way of your message and as a result your message is more apt to be clear.

As you become more skilled, your style can vary for different types of letters. Ideally, you should choose your words and phrases to fit your audience and your occasion, exactly as you would if you were giving a speech. That lets your readers know you're talking specifically to *them*, not just *anyone*.

HOW DOES TONE DIFFER FROM STYLE?

What specifically is tone? Tone is the emotional atmosphere that surrounds your writing style, that evokes emotional responses in readers.

Your style of writing, the inflections, mood, level of formality or informality you use in communicating, all affect the tone of your letters. The tone you employ with the president of your company might not work as well for your closest colleague.

Tone is just as important in writing as it is in speaking. As in writing a marketing document, you're selling yourself, your company, and your ideas, so keep your tone upbeat, positive and warm. That will market both you and your topic most favorably.

The tone of a letter you write will often reflect the attitude you have about the topic to begin with. If you are angry when you write, for example, your feelings will be more likely to come through in your communication. Look at the next two sample letters in this chapter. Pay attention to how the writer (the same person wrote both letters) has adjusted the tone to fit the audience.

March 2, 19XX

Ms. Sara Shamblin
Address
City, State ZIP

Subject: CORPORATE ADVERTISING

Dear Ms. Shamblin:

We have had occasions to use the corporate advertising group to reprint several pieces of promotional litera-ture recently. As you can see from the attached analy-ses, in each case there has been a substantial penalty to Concepts, Inc. for having materials printed in-house.

In the case of the distributor products catalog, the half we are charged is competitive with commercial rates, but the total cost to Concepts, Inc., including what was picked up in Lee's budget, was substan-tially higher. We have already committed to the corporate advertising group to have several other pieces printed and will, of course, honor those commit-ments; however, unless you have strong feelings to the contrary, we will plan to do future printing locally. We will get quotes from the corporate group periodically to ensure that the economics have not changed.

Sincerely,

Betty Shearer

cc: Allen Miller

March 30, 19XX

Mr. Allen Miller
Address
City, State ZIP

Subject: SALES CONFERENCE

Dear Mr. Miller:

I think the Sales Conference will be a useful time to
get a feel for our business from the people in the
field. An agenda is attached for your information.

I have asked Kathy, my assistant, to check your
schedule, as well as Cue's, to see if we can hold our
Board of Directors meeting on the 8th before the
conference dinner.

I'll be in touch on details when I return to the office
on April 23.

Sincerely,

Betty Shearer

cc: Sara Shamblin

    The second letter has a more informal and congenial
tone. The writer uses personal pronouns, consciously includes the audience in her text, and breaks the information up into smaller, more easily readable paragraphs.
    If you're uncertain about tone, consider your mood.
Mood often is the same as tone. The only problem with
keeping them parallel is that you might be in an unpleasant mood, yet have to write a letter in a friendly or
respectful tone. It's important not to let your mood of the
moment influence your tone in a letter.
    For instance, a supervisor asks you to write a letter on
very short notice. You aren't in a good mood so you don't
want to write the letter, but she's your supervisor, so you
have to. Now, it is preferable to write that letter in an

upbeat rather than resentful manner. Express your displeasure in another way, not in a letter that carries your signature and affects your reputation. Too many people let their feelings leak out in inappropriate places in their writing. Such a lapse can cloud your communication and cause problems for your career. These negative letters have been known to find a permanent place in the writer's employee file—just where you don't want them.

Another word for tone is attitude. Let's say you have a positive attitude that comes across in a readable, likable way in your letters. That's a highly desirable, rare asset. But suppose your attitude on a particular day isn't very positive. You cast pessimism or resentment into your letters. Your readers can see beneath your words. The slightest tinge of negativity can cause an unfavorable reaction. You want that letter to be positive and professional, and therefore, you have to write as if it were the most important message you've ever written in your life.

The tones that work best in business writing are the same ones that work well in relationships: warm, upbeat, positive, friendly, enthusiastic. Since your writing is your ambassador on paper, it's critical that you project a positive image.

WORDS THAT CREATE EMOTIONAL RESPONSES

Some words tend to create a *negative* response among readers when used, so should be avoided:

apology	careless	disagreement
biased	curt	disaster
blame	death	dislike
blunt	defeat	failure

fault	never	suspicion
fear	not	trickery
hesitant	prohibit	uncomfortable
inconvenient	refusal	unfair
lazy	regret	unfortunate
must	reject	untimely
neglect	selfish	weak
negligence	sorry	wrong

Some words tend to create a *positive* response among readers when used, so should be used. A sample of such positive words include:

ability	courtesy	loyalty
accuracy	desire (to serve)	pleased
adjustment	diplomacy	right
admirable	distinction	substantial
ambition	effective	tact
assurance	fair	thoughtful
benefit	faith	understanding
calm	generous	useful
commendable	glad	willing
confidence	good	wise
cooperation	happy	

CHAPTER 9

Writing Powerful Business Letters

DIRECT LETTERS

INDIRECT LETTERS

PERSUASIVE LETTERS

It's now time to put all we have discussed into practice. In this section we will discuss three broad types of letters: direct, indirect, and persuasive.

DIRECT LETTERS

Direct letters are one of the most common types of business letters written. Direct letters are straightforward and concise in the way they explain and ask for something. These letters include good-news letters, letters of inquiry, letters of credit, letters of complaint, and letters of adjustment.

GOOD-NEWS LETTERS

Good-news letters are basically that—letters that provide positive news. They award jobs, contracts, grants, requests, promotions, or make special commendations. These letters are enjoyable. We all like imparting good news. Here are rules for good-news letters.

○ Begin the letter with congratulations. Make your message positive!

○ Show why you're happy. How does it help you, your company, and your employees? Be specific. You want to convince your reader that you mean what you say.

○ Provide any qualifications. These are the "ifs" and "buts." For example, when you award a contract to someone, state the major stipulations or changes. For example, if you've just offered someone a promotion, and ten-hour workdays accompany the promotion, this is the place to state that qualification.

○ State the results you expect. What do you want your reader to do to accept your offer? Sign a contract? Call you? Answer you with a letter? Tell your reader what you want.

○ Close the letter by briefly restating the good news. Reiterate your happiness.

GOOD-NEWS LETTERS

○ Start with positive message

○ Specifically explain why you're pleased

○ Provide "ifs" and "buts" if needed

○ State results that you expect

○ Close with recap

SAMPLE GOOD-NEWS LETTER

April 14, 19XX

Mr. John Walker, President
San Diego Construction Co., Inc.
5489 Seaside Drive
San Diego, CA 92101

Dear Mr. Walker:

Congratulations on being awarded the first Ocean
Way Condominium project! The competition was
tough. It was a difficult decision, but we feel we've
picked the best company for the job!

Let's schedule a meeting to launch the project. It'll
be a nice way for our companies to meet. Let me
know when it's convenient; Thursday is good for us.

I'm looking forward to working with you and San
Diego Construction.

Sincerely,

J.P. Forbes
President
ABC COMPANY

JPF/jss

cc: M. Floyd
    C. Miller

LETTERS OF INQUIRY

This type letter is used when you have a simple request that in all likelihood will be granted. Start by coming to the point and stating your request. Then state the reasons for your request, providing detail and justification as necessary. Close the letter courteously with a note of appreciation. Be specific as to when you need your request satisfied if this is not awkward to state.

SAMPLE LETTER OF INQUIRY

Advanced Engineering and
Management Corporation
1786 Nobel Way
Ithaca, NY 16483

September 19, 19XX

Mr. Ben Forsyth
Sales Manager
The Computer Warehouse
Oxnard, OH

Dear Mr. Forsyth:

When you were here last week, you mentioned some upcoming dBASE III seminars. Please send us the fall seminar schedule. Our logisticians would like to manage their own database, and I am responsible for creating a resume database of the employees at all our facilities. Therefore, three of us are interested in taking your dBase III seminar.

Thanks for your continued support. We are growing so fast that we need all the assistance we can get in adapting ourselves, as well as our equipment, to our changing requirements.

Sincerely,

Delores Smith
Department of Quality Assurance
Advanced Engineering and Management Corporation

LETTERS OF INQUIRY
(Direct Pattern)

Opening: Clear statement of inquiry
                 or request

Middle: Necessary explanation and
                 supporting details

Closing: Expression of appreciation
                 and date by which reply
                 is needed

REPLY TO LETTERS OF INQUIRY
(Direct Pattern)

Opening: Direct response if
                 good news

Middle: Supporting explanation
                 as needed

Closing: Cordial, concise close

LETTERS OF CREDIT

A letter of credit is similar to other direct letters, but requires a bit more substantiation in order to justify the request for credit. You need to provide the information needed, typically your monthly income and debts, in order for the reader to make a favorable decision. In most requests for credit, you will need to complete an application, so your letter should simply request such an application or serve as a cover letter for an application.

LETTERS OF CREDIT

○ Specifically request the amount needed

○ Justify your request by providing your monthly income and debt

○ State the next action you expect

○ Request application if needed

SAMPLE LETTER OF CREDIT

October 7, 19XX

MAJORBANK VISA
Manager of Credit
P.O. Box 6000
Sioux Falls, SD 57117-6000

Subject: CREDIT LIMIT FOR VISA XXX-XXX-XXX-XXX

Gentlemen:

My Visa card's credit limit needs to be at least
$10,000.

Over the last ten years I have used the American
Express card for both business travel and personal
purchases. I ordered the "AAdvantage" Visa card in
July 19XX with the intention of using only that card
for future credit purchases. However, my extensive
business travel leaves me concerned. Will I be caught
short (or embarrassed) on one of my trips? Therefore, I request an increase in my current credit limit
of $5,000. To help you evaluate my credit status, I
will complete a financial statement.

Without an increase in my current limit, I will be
unable to use your Visa card for my business travel.
Thank you for considering this matter.

Sincerely,

John Schnieder

SAMPLE LETTER OF CREDIT

August 14, 19XX

Mr. John Sims
Credit Manager
ABC Furniture Store
769 Broadway Avenue
Miami, FL

Dear Mr. Sims:

I am writing to request installment credit with your company. I am currently employed by Applications Scientists International in Miami, Florida and have been so employed since May 4, 19XX. My present position is Systems and Placement Coordinator and my annual salary is $47,000.

I live in a rented apartment that costs $520 per month, and have a car payment of $238/month, utility bills of approximately $150/month, and a Sears bill of about $50/month. After meeting these expenses, my current salary would easily allow me to make a monthly payment to you on the living-room set.

Please send me a credit application or whatever other paperwork is necessary to open an installment charge with your firm.

I look forward to your prompt response and our future business dealings.

Sincerely,

Jackie Simon

LETTERS OF ADJUSTMENT

Sometimes mistakes occur that need to be identified and corrected as expediently as possible. In this case a letter of adjustment is needed. Work from the facts to explain as precisely as you can what is wrong and how the situation can be corrected. We've included two sample letters of adjustment—a simple one and a more involved letter.

SAMPLE LETTER OF ADJUSTMENT

1068 Hornblend Street
Ann Arbor, Michigan

October 14, 19XX

ABC Catalog
1100 West 36th Street
Chicago, IL 60667

Attention: Billing Department

Dear Billing Department Manager:

Enclosed is a copy of an invoice dated July 30, 19XX. An error in billing has been made in that I was charged for merchandise that I did not order.

Item Number Z0325 for $34 was inadvertently posted on my bill, bringing the total balance due to $148.50. I have enclosed a check for $114.50 for the difference due. Please adjust my account accordingly. Thank you.

Sincerely,

Cynthia G. Sharp

Enclosures

SAMPLE LETTER OF ADJUSTMENT

February 16, 19XX

Manager of Customer Relations
ENTERTAINMENT CRUISES
1202 "B" Street
San Diego, CA 92101

Dear Manager:

On Valentine's Day, my spouse and I and two couples from out-of-town took your evening dinner cruise. This was the fifth time that we have attended your dinner cruise, and we have also referred other friends and visiting company. Unless reparations are made, however, that cruise will be our last.

Due to many factors, the evening was a disaster. Our party of six was assigned to Table M-28, a table for two. After repeated discussions with three of your crew members, no corrective action was taken to seat us properly so we finally just found a remote table. The Showboat appeared to be overbooked and the crowd made it difficult for us to hear each other talk, let alone move about on board. I was repeatedly bumped by both other guests and servers during dinner. Our dinners were not served until past 9:30 p.m., they were not served hot, nor were they properly cooked. Dessert was not served until very close to docking. Time left for scenic viewing was very limited and the decks were so crowded as to make such viewing unpleasant.

Any one of these factors might easily have been tolerable; together they effectively destroyed the "special occasion" we had hoped to experience and had promised our guests. At the premium prices you charge, I feel especially mistreated.

Although you can never restore our evening nor alter the memory that it left us, I feel that some type of financial reimbursement would be in order—especially if we are to use or refer others to your cruises again. Enclosed is the receipt for $180 I spent. I would appreciate hearing from you soon.

Sincerely,

Robert B. Nelson
9993 Avenida Magnifica
San Diego, CA 92131

RESPONSE TO LETTER OF ADJUSTMENT

February 19, 19XX

Mr. Robert B. Nelson
9993 Avenida Magnifica
San Diego, CA 92131

Dear Mr. Nelson:

Thank you for your letter of February 16, 19XX.
Valentine's Day is a special, sentimental day. I apologize that this will not be one that you will look back
on with the fondest of memories.

We were and are aware of the problems that arose on
Sunday. You are right — it was not a smooth evening.
We had several employees who did not show up to
work. Coupled with some miscommunication in
reservations, that made for a chaotic evening.

I can assure you that corrective measures are being
taken. The boat is undergoing structural changes
that will enhance dining space, create added mobil-
ity, and protect against overcrowding. We have hired
and are in the process of training new staff. We are
also changing our menu. In the future we will be
offering a choice of a prime rib'or swordfish dinner.

So often, in all areas of the hospitality industry,
unhappy experiences are not reported. We welcome
your feedback. It is due to your concern that high
standards and quality can become more consistent.

I am enclosing a gift certificate for six people. I
regret the disappointment that you have encoun-
tered, and hope to see you again *enjoying* yourself on
our beautiful bay.

Please be our guest soon.

Sincerely,

Judith Gower
Cruise Director
Entertainment Cruises

```
┌─────────────────────────────────────────────┐
│                                             │
│          LETTERS OF ADJUSTMENT              │
│                                             │
│   ○  Stick to the facts                     │
│                                             │
│   ○  Be precise about what happened         │
│                                             │
│   ○  Be precise about the correction        │
│      you desire                             │
│                                             │
│   ○  End on a positive note                 │
│                                             │
└─────────────────────────────────────────────┘
```

LETTERS OF COMPLAINT

Have you ever accepted poor quality or service in a product you purchased simply because you didn't take the time to write a letter of complaint? If so, you're in the majority. Writing this type of letter doesn't have to be drudgery. You can make it short and to the point, and obtain results. Assertive business practice often dictates that you write this type of letter.

Rule one regarding letters of complaint: *never* angrily complain in a complaint letter. If you are hostile and rude, what kind of results do you think you will get? If you answered "none," you're right! Most people, when confronted in this manner, get defensive and angry. Consider the sample we call "An Overly Emotional Letter of Complaint," on page 138.

Obviously, John Thomas wrote this letter in anger and frustration. Although he doesn't threaten, he also doesn't say what he wants. It's important to tell the reader what you want.

Rule two regarding letters of complaint: ask for what you want. Read the rewrite of Mr. Thomas' letter: "An Improved Letter of Complaint." Notice the change in

AN OVERLY EMOTIONAL
LETTER OF COMPLAINT

Dear Sir:

I'm very disappointed in the computer I bought from
you last week. The hard disk crashes every time I use
it. I called your service representative three times
before he returned my calls. He finally came out on a
service call but said he could find nothing wrong
with it and that it was probably "user error"! Nevertheless, when I started using it again, it crashed
once more!

I am hoping that I can obtain some satisfaction after
all the inconvenience I have been caused. I expect to
hear from you shortly.

Yours truly,

John Thomas

tone. The letter is also more factual and organized, and the writer states what action he expects from the computer dealer.

In letters of complaint, your tone is crucial. Never appear angry, hostile, vindictive, or threatening when you write your letter. Let it sit for twenty-four hours before you mail it—better yet, have a colleague read it.

Avoid terms such as *complaint, rotten, lemon, disgusted, dishonest, false, untrue,* or other such harsh and negative terms. Be professional. Here are some specific guidelines for writing complaint letters:

○ Start with an explanation of the problem. Be specific and use dates, amounts, model numbers, and any other concrete information when possible and where appropriate. Use a positive tone and be complimentary about something, if possible.

○ State your inconvenience or loss as succinctly as possible. Again, use dates, amounts, and other documenting information. Stick to the facts and avoid emotions.

○ State the results or action you expect. This principle is the same as in any business letter. Let your reader know what you want. Avoid threats, such as a loss of business, especially if this is your first communication regarding the problem. You can always threaten later if you must. However, you should reserve this type of communication for your final action.

○ Close in a friendly manner. Indicate that you trust the company and welcome its help. Appeal to the company's desire to retain you as a customer and to maintain its reputation for strong customer service.

AN IMPROVED LETTER OF COMPLAINT

Dear Regional Manager:

On June 28, 1987, I purchased an ABC computer, Model D, with a 40 Megabyte hard disk drive from your Phoenix store. I purchased the ABC because of its excellent record, and I bought it from Computerville because of your reputation for service and customer concern.

Unfortunately, the computer has malfunctioned, causing me considerable inconvenience and frustration. Following is a sequence of dates and contacts that describe the problem and actions taken to resolve it.

- June 30, 1987 — I called your store and requested service. (I have purchased the service agreement.)
- July 2 — The service representative came to my home, checked the drive, and fixed it.
- July 15 — The drive malfunctioned again. I lost half my data. I called the service representative. He came and picked up the drive and took it into the shop for repair. I was without the use of my computer for two days.
- July 27 — The service representative returned my drive. It worked well for three days.
- July 30 — Again the drive malfunctioned, and again I lost data. Note that it has only been a month since I purchased the computer.

In view of my inconvenience, I am asking that you replace this hard drive as soon as possible. As I urgently need the use of this computer for my business, I would also appreciate a loaner until I can be assured that my machine is in sound working condition.

Sincerely,

John Thomas

When you follow these guidelines, you emphasize the *facts* of the situation rather than your emotions. You appeal to your reader's business sense; it's good business to have satisfied customers. Also, you let the reader determine the specific adjustment appropriate for your situation. It may be enough to state that you do expect some satisfaction or compensation.

LETTERS OF COMPLAINT

○ Start with explanation of problem

○ State inconvenience to you

○ State specific results or action you expect

○ Close in a friendly manner

INDIRECT LETTERS

Indirect letters are used when you are communicating information that is in some way unpleasant to the reader. While, in general, good business writing is concise, studies indicate that when short letters contain negative information, readers often feel slighted, as if their request was not given appropriate consideration. To avoid offending the readers, professional letters that communicate negative news should be as positive or neutral as possible.

BAD-NEWS LETTERS

Too many letters that have bad news start with such phrases as: "Unfortunately . . . ," "It is with regret . . . ," or "We are sorry. . . ." Often such letters once again remind the reader of the unpleasantness of the letter at the close as well: "Regretting this inconvenience . . . ," "We are sorry that this is the case. . . ," or "Again accept our apologies for our inability . . . ."

Such letters are twice sad! They are sad at the beginning because they signal the reader to *watch* for "bad news" and again at the end because they *remind* the reader of the "bad news."

Not every letter can bear good news. Unfortunate circumstances do occur, adjustments and requests have to be refused, applications must be denied, job hunters must be turned away. When such a situation arises, most writers are prone to start by getting directly to the point, as we have previously advocated. And writers often feel it would be better to use such words as "sorry" and "unfortunately" and "regret" to "buffer" the message.

It is better to have your business correspondence be as positive as possible as often as possible. If you look hard enough there is usually some kind of "good news" that can be emphasized. For instance, here is a typical turndown letter:

> Unfortunately, we cannot supply you with the dozen cases of compound that you recently ordered. We are sorry that this is the case, but circumstances beyond our control . . .
>
> However, if you could get by with three cases, we'll do our best to ship these to you . . .

The "good news" is buried. Why not turn the letter around so it reads:

> We'll be glad to ship you three cases of compound . . .
> we wish we could send you the 12 you requested. . . .

Put the good news first! Then proceed with the "ifs" and "buts" and "howevers." Let the turndown wait until later in the letter when the reader has been cushioned for the shock.

Suppose there is no good news? At least you can *wish* there were! You can at least start the letter on a positive note by thanking the other person for writing and then you can say something like:

> We wish we could . . . but . . .
>
> Much as we would like to . . . but since . . .
>
> Nothing would give us more pleasure than to . . . however. . . .

These phrases soften the bad news. Then you can proceed with the negative information, giving a convincing explanation of why the request must be denied. Finally, instead of ending the letter with a "regret" or an "apology," you can close on a constructive note for the future.

A POOR BAD-NEWS LETTER EXCERPT

> We are very sorry that we will be unable to fill your order for Book No. 1, as the instock date was changed to the latter part of May.
>
> The reason for the delay is that we had to make some last-minute changes in this book, and as a result the book is being held at the printer.
>
> We have entered an order for Book No. 2 for immediate shipment to you.
>
> Please accept our apologies for the inconvenience we have caused you in the delay.

"Sorrys," "apologies," "inconvenience" . . . how sad! And the "good news" is buried in the third paragraph. Why not turn the letter around?

AN IMPROVED BAD-NEWS LETTER EXCERPT

Thank you for your order for Books 1 and 2.

You'll be glad to know Book No. 2 is being immediately shipped to you. I am sure this book will make
many pleasant hours of profitable reading.

Book No. 1 will be sent to you shortly. We had some last
minute changes on this book, and it is now at the
printer. But I'm sure you'll agree when you read it that
these changes make the book well worth waiting for.

As soon as Book No. 1 is off the presses—which
should be in about six weeks from now—your copy
will be rushed to you.

There is no excuse for a curt, indifferent turndown letter.
Letters can say an emphatic "no"—but they can say it in a
way that wins customer goodwill.

DEVELOPING BAD-NEWS LETTERS

1. Start with something good,
   partially good, or pleasing, relevant,
   and neutral

2. Tell the reader what can be done

3. If nothing can be done, soften the
   "no" with a phrase such as "I wish I
   could . . . but . . . "

4. Explain why something can't be
   done; don't hide behind company
   policy or blame others

5. End letter on constructive note
   - Suggest alternative
   - Appreciate reader's interest
   - Offer future assustance

SAMPLE BAD-NEWS LETTER

ABC TRAVEL
1932 Oceanside Terrace
Hermosa Beach, CA 92973

October 21, 19XX

Ms. Renee Sanders
1556 Adams Avenue
Whittier, CA 93475

Dear Ms. Sanders:

Thank you for sending the details of your trip to Italy.

Before accepting your deposit check confirming the itinerary for your trip, I explained the hotel accommodations I had arranged. You will recall you specifically requested a room near the Piazza San Marco in Venice. My letter to you of June 4 explained that a room in that location at the price you were willing to pay would not have a bath.

Please accept the enclosed book, *Foreign Travel Facts*, with my compliments. This is a new publication. I believe it provides helpful background information for anyone planning foreign travel.

Thank you again for sharing the good news about your trip. I look forward to arranging more adventures for you.

Sincerely,

Lois L. Schmidt
Owner/Agent

Enclosure

LETTERS OF REJECTION

A subset of "bad-news" letters are letters of rejection. Rejection letters contain negative information. These are the letters we often postpone and sometimes never quite get around to writing. Examples of rejection letters include rejections of job applicants, proposals, promotions, or manuscripts. In writing a rejection letter, be clear in expressing your decision without overly focusing on the negative.

Here are our guidelines for writing rejection letters:

○ Begin your rejection letters by opening with praise. Let your reader know you care, and acknowledge that you understand his or her problem.

○ State your decision concisely, directly, and firmly. Don't leave room for doubt. Be kind and gentle at the same time. Tone is extremely important in this type of letter. Never be hostile; instead be sensitive, warm, and caring.

○ State your reasons. You may be able to include this information in the previous paragraph. Again, be kind, but firm. Let the reader know your decision was a difficult one.

○ Follow up with further explanations and any alternatives. For example, if you're rejecting a job applicant, tell the applicant that you're keeping his or her application on file for six months in case any openings occur, or that you'll direct his or her application to another department that would be more suitable to the applicant's talents. Make your reader feel better in this paragraph without offering false hope. One friend of ours related his reaction to his first rejection letter from a major publisher. The negativity of the letter devastated him so much that he actually gave up writing for an entire year! Finally, he submitted a second manuscript to another publisher. Although they also rejected him, the letter he received was positive. He felt encouraged and optimistic. He kept writing. Today he is a successfully published author.

○ Close on a positive note. Don't repeat the rejection. Offer best wishes and tell your reader that you sincerely hope that things work out.

SAMPLE LETTER OF REJECTION

May 23, 19XX

Mr. Jack Fielding
6785 North Spauling Avenue
San Francisco, CA 94545

Dear Mr. Fielding:

We received your application for the Project Manager
position at ABC Company, and have reviewed your
background against our current needs. Although
you have excellent qualifications, we have filled the
position with someone who has more directly
related experience.

We are continuing to grow, and opportunities that
more closely match your qualifications may arise in
the future. We therefore plan to keep your resume on
hand in anticipation of our future needs. If an appropriate position becomes available, we will call you for
an interview.

In the meantime, we wish you well in your job
search and thank you for your interest in the
ABC Company.

Sincerely,

Josephine V. Thomas
Vice President
Human Resources Department

JVT/jss

LETTERS OF APOLOGY

Suppose you have made an error with a customer's account or you receive a letter of complaint. How shall you respond? First, answer it promptly, no matter how inconsequential or offensive it seems to you. If your customer spent the time writing, the letter deserves your response. Your answer should be polite, fair, and logical. Avoid getting defensive or angry, no matter what the tone of the complaint letter.

Here are some additional guidelines for responses to such letters:

○ Begin positively. State the good news immediately if there is any. If not, make some positive statement, such as, "It pleases us that you decided to purchase your first computer from Computerville."

○ Offer a factual explanation of the events leading to the problem. Be specific, concise, and direct. Never over-defend yourself, yet don't blame the customer.

○ The customer is always right. Remember the business edict "the customer is always right." Tell your customer the adjustment you are willing to make. If it's not what the customer requested, explain why in factual terms. Apologize, and at the same time, emphasize the positive aspects of your adjustment.

○ Close with good will. Resell your good name, product, service, and company. Tell them you value them as customers. Their business is important to you.

Look at the sample letter of apology and the friendly rewrite. Which do you prefer?

POOR LETTER OF APOLOGY

Dear Mr. Thomas:

We are sorry that we cannot satisfy your request.
Unfortunately, our company's policy has always been
one of "let the buyer beware." That's why we can
keep our prices low.

We do offer a ten-day return policy.

However, since you have exceeded the time limit,
there is really nothing I can do.

Sincerely,

George C. West
General Manager

IMPROVED LETTER OF APOLOGY

Dear Mr. Thomas:

We will be glad to replace your hard disk as soon as
possible. We are sorry for your trouble and inconvenience. There has been a bad shipment of hard drives
installed in some of the ABC's Model D's. You're
quite right in expecting better service from our store,
especially since Computerville bases its reputation on
customer service.

We don't have any Model D's available for a "loaner,"
but we do have Model C's and Model B's. If they
can't do the job, perhaps we can provide you with
Computerville's own brand, which is comparable to
the Model D.

Please call me as soon as possible to arrange for
service and a replacement computer. You are a
valued Computerville customer. We want to make
your every transaction satisfactory, and we hope to
resolve this situation soon.

Sincerely,

George T. West
General Manager

LETTERS OF APOLOGY

1. Begin positively, providing an immediate "fix" to the problem

2. Apologize only once; keep negative words to a maximum of three

3. Offer a factual explanation, giving customers the benefit of the doubt

4. Provide permanent "fix" if possible; assure reader all possible steps are being taken to prevent reoccurrence

5. Don't pass the buck if it's really yours; accept the blame (where necessary, check with your legal department first)

6. End letter on a positive note that builds goodwill

PERSUASIVE LETTERS

The final broad type of business letter is the persuasive letter. This letter not only presents information to the reader, but also seeks to convince the reader to take a certain action. Such letters typically rely on more than just a statement of fact to persuade a reader; they must also be logical and possible — where appropriate, playing on the reader's emotions. Sales letters, job-hunting correspondence, and recommendations are typical examples of persuasive letters.

Persuasive letters tend to be longer than direct or indirect letters. A typical persuasive letter first seeks to

SAMPLE PERSUASIVE LETTER

January 12, 19XX

Mrs. Sandra Kopple
273 South Pleasant Lane
Buffalo, NY 17456

Dear Mrs. Kopple:

It's a hot summer day in 1945. Paul's friends have invited him over to cool off in their swimming pool but he can't go. The possibility of catching the polio virus is too frightening.

Today our children are more fortunate. The polio vaccine is available. But what made this vaccine possible?

Basic medical research. The kind of difficult, frustrating, often tedious research that produces answers where there didn't seem to be any. The kind of work conducted at the Rochester Research Institute.

As one of the largest private research centers in America, the Research Institute continues to advance biomedical research. By studying immunology, molecular biology, and now neurobiology as well, our scientists are unraveling the mysteries of disease. What is discovered today will lead to the cures of tomorrow.

But we need your help.

For only $14 a month, *you can make a difference* in our search for answers. Your pledge makes you a member of the Research Council. It is a tax-deductible contribution that helps us carry on this vital work.

As a member, you will receive our bimonthly *Special Research Report*. Each issue focuses on a specific area of concern and study at the Institute. Cancer, Alzheimer's disease, arthritis, the effects of drugs and alcohol on the brain—each is discussed in light of the latest research findings.

You also will be invited to attend special programs sponsored by the Rochester Research Foundation. Experts in the field make presentations and are available to answer your questions.

Help support the Research Institute in its commitment to discover the critical information that will lead to long-awaited cures. Please accept my personal invitation to become a Council member. Simply complete the enclosed card and return it today with your check or credit card number. Make your pledge today.

Sincerely,

Christopher Chapman
Chairman

p.s.: Your support is vital to the advancement of medical research. Join the Research Council and share in the discoveries that will allow us to triumph over disease.

PERSUASIVE LETTERS
(THAT ASK FOR FAVORS)

1. Attract attention

2. Specify details; tell reader
   necessary facts to
   make decision

3. State request and tell why it is
   important to you

4. If necessary, tell reader why you
   selected him/her

5. Motivate action; tell what you want
   reader to do

6. Make it easy to reply

7. Close cordially; offer to
   return favor

---

grab the reader's attention, perhaps by beginning with a statistic, question, or example. The body of the letter then builds upon the initial interest that has been created. An attempt is made to first create a desire to act, and then a conviction to act, on the part of the reader.

SALES LETTERS

A common persuasive letter is the sales letter. Every person at one time or another is selling something. This might be a product or service or a proposal or raise. To be persuasive, you need to capture your reader's attention, keep it, and get your reader to take the action you desire.

We advocate the following guidelines for writing effective sales letters:

○ *Attract your reader's attention.* Shock them. Appeal to their self-interest and pride. Hook them. These are techniques Madison Avenue advertisers use successfully to entice us to buy luxury items we believe we have to own. The fact that we've been living without them suddenly disappears. Advertisers notoriously use dramatic, attention-getting ads. You might open with a question. Remember, sales promotion letters can overwhelm and get thrown out as soon as they're opened. Your sales letter must attract, yet be pertinent to your audience. State the advantages of your products and services. Look at the letter excerpt below. It appears to have all the elements of an effective sales letter, yet it doesn't overwhelm the reader.

> What does Laguna San Rafael Resort and Spa Offer the investor?
>
> The opportunity to be part of this luxurious, exciting resort. You invest only in the ownership of your suite, but you can enjoy *all* the benefits of a premiere destination resort.

You need to know your audience; what seems like an advantage to you might appear as a disadvantage to them. For example, you wouldn't want to try and sell a sports car to an audience consisting of large families unless you specify it could be a good "second" or "fun" car.

○ *Create desire*. Make them want what you have to sell. Show them how their life will improve if they buy your product or service. Remember that the advantages must outweigh the costs. Look at the next excerpt. The writer knows his audience is a beach property owner. He is appealing to his reader's values as an owner of real estate.

As an owner of a Newport Beach apartment house, you can appreciate the area and its value. I'm proud to currently have exclusively listed one of the finest buildings in Newport Beach.

The property's superior location is on Beach Street, within four blocks of the beach. Only "pride of owner-ship" can describe this building. Built fourteen years ago, this one-owner property has had meticulous care both inside and out.

○ *Persuade*. This is the "sell." Use facts, statistics, logic, or expert testimony. If you use "expert" testimony, make sure your experts are knowledgeable about your product and not just someone famous. Many television commercials ignore this principle, but get away with it due to the fame of their experts—for example, famous Hollywood stars are used to sell soft drinks. You probably won't pay millions of dollars for your experts, so use real experts to "tell your truth." But make that truth believable. Otherwise, you'll lose your credibility and potential customers.

Have you ever received one of those envelopes that promise millions of dollars if you only fill out the coupon and send it in? They guarantee you're a winner! Do you believe them? If you're like most

extremely busy executives, chances are you dump
these envelopes in your trash without even opening
them. Do you worry that you've thrown away a
million dollars? Of course not. These claims are so
outrageous that you don't believe them. As a matter
of fact, you even get irritated that the sender has
thought you're foolish to believe such mockery!
Truth is persuasive; exaggeration is not.

○ *Action*. Tell them what you want them to do,
how to do it, and when to do it. Be as specific
as possible. Don't say, "Please call at your
earliest convenience." Instead, say, "Please
call 555-5000 by July 1."

Following are three more excerpts from sales letters.
What are the qualities of the effective sales letters? What
are the mistakes of the ineffective ones?

The first letter is geared toward business executives
who might subscribe to a magazine. It is dry and boring
and loses its reader in the first sentence.

> **Poor:** We would like to take this opportunity to
> announce a new magazine especially for business
> executives. You will find many interesting sections
> that are particularly geared to the problems and
> concerns of business people across the continent.
> Our readership includes all type of businesses. . . .

The next two excerpts combine much of the elements
we've discussed. They have effective openings and contain
all the necessary elements to keep readers' interest. The
excerpt is directed toward a potential real estate investor:

Good: Do you like the idea of making money while you sleep? If so, please take a minute to look at this exciting investment opportunity. The owners of this Fallbrook property had planned to develop the sites but the partnership recently decided to sell instead.

The land/value price is underpriced considerably. We think this area will be another Mission Valley within the next two years.

The last excerpt is geared to potential luxury car owners:

Good: We have an exciting job ahead. It's our privilege to introduce a new Italian touring sedan to American drivers. Its name is Panther. It's sleek, fast, and projects a boldness seldom seen within the staid European automotive establishment. The Panther combines it driver-oriented technology with a level of comfort designed to be unmatched by other vehicles in its class.

SALES LETTERS

OPENING:	A relevant idea that will grab the reader's attention and cause him or her to continue reading
MIDDLE: (Interest Desire Conviction)	Develop opening idea through explanation of what is needed, leading directly to outright request whenever it fits logically and naturally
CLOSING: (Action)	Specific courteous request for desired response

EMPLOYMENT LETTERS

Letters used in obtaining employment are another type of persuasive letter. There are hundreds of excellent books on job hunting (see the references cited in Appendix C), so our discussion here will be brief. Cover letters, the resume, letters of recommendation, and thank-you letters are all commonly used in job hunting.

COVER LETTERS.   A cover letter accompanies a resume when it is sent to employers. The purpose of a cover letter and resume is to get an interview. Toward this end, you want to present only the best qualifications and relevant information you have for the position you are seeking. The cover letter should be brief, starting with an attention getter about yourself, then highlighting a few items on your resume (and in the process, drawing the reader to the resume). It should ideally be addressed to a person you have spoken with about the possibility of employment. It should close with an action *you intend to take* as a next step, typically to contact the addressee in a week or less.

THE COVER LETTER

○ Impressive fact about yourself

○ Two or three most relevant qualifications for the position you are seeking

○ Tie in to the resume

○ Action you will next take to follow up

SAMPLE COVER LETTER

November 22, 19XX

Mr. John Doe
Executive Director
RESEARCH INSTITUTE OF AMERICA
123 State Street
Sacramento, CA 95647

Dear Mr. Doe:

Mr. John Gilman, whom I work with as a fellow NSPRE board member, mentioned your need for a special-events director. I have spent much of my career creating, organizing, and marketing special events and thus feel I am an excellent candidate for this position. Special events are really people events. From the planning stages to attendance, successful events require cooperation, enthusiasm, and the involvement of many people.

Enclosed is my resume, indicating that my strong interpersonal and organizational skills have been a major factor in the many successful events I have directed. I am very interested in using these skills at an organization like yours.

Thank you for your time. I would like to meet at your convenience to discuss this position and will call you next week to arrange a time.

Sincerely,

Sandra J. Beverly
enclosure

THE RESUME. The resume is basically a one-page advertisement about yourself. It should contain only the most relevant and recent job experience, qualifications, and education history for the job you are seeking. There are several types of resume formats. You should select a format that best represents you on paper. A sample of the traditional resume format is presented on the next page.

TRADITIONAL RESUME FORMAT

Sandra J. Beverly
7650 Arrow Wood Hills
La Jolla, CA 92037
(619) 555-9999

PROFESSIONAL OBJECTIVE

Professional position that challenges my organizational and interpersonal skills in a human services organization.

SUMMARY OF SKILLS

Extensive experience in annual fund-raising with an emphasis on direct mail campaigns. Strong interpersonal skills developed through working with donors, volunteers, staff members, and consultants.

EXPERIENCE

Director of Annual Giving   December 1983-present
SCRIPPS CLINIC AND RESEARCH FOUNDATION, La Jolla, CA
Promoted to this position. Have raised over $2.5 million through direct mail donor acquisition, renewal, and upgrade programs. Over 1.2 million pieces mailed annually. Major focus: donor communications and recognition, special events, and volunteer coordination.

Development Office Coordinator   July 1981-Nov. 1983
SCRIPPS CLINIC AND RESEARCH FOUNDATION, La Jolla, CA
Promoted to this position. Steady interaction with other departments and outside vendors. Prepared and managed operating budget. Word processing supervisor and trainer. Coordinated donor recognition and special projects.

Donations Secretary   March 1980-June 1981
SCRIPPS CLINIC AND RESEARCH FOUNDATION, La Jolla, CA
Prepared gift receipts. Calculated and produced monthly gifts and grants report. Donor file and record maintenance. Word processing.

Direct Mail Manager   September 1978-March 1980
THE INNOVATION GROUP, La Jolla, CA Researched and compiled lists of national corporations. Word processing. Direct mail production and management. Secretarial duties.

EDUCATION

UCSD Extension   San Diego, CA Fall 1987
Courses in Business Writing and Public Relations

The Fund Raising School   Oakland, CA June 1985
Introductory course in fundraising

PROFESSIONAL DEVELOPMENT

San Diego Direct Marketing Club   Member 1987

NSFRE   Member 1983—present
Treasurer-elect 1988
Philanthropy Awards Chairman 1987
Nominating Committee 1986—1987
Fundraising Day Program Co-chair 1986
Newsletter Committee 1983—1986

November 19XX

THANK-YOU LETTERS.   A simple, short, sincere thank-you letter can go far in showing a potential employer that you are still very interested in a job for which you've interviewed, and that you are a well-mannered, high-initiative individual who can communicate effectively. Job hunting studies have highly correlated the activity of writing thank-you letters with successfully finding employment. A good thank-you letter will thank the interviewer, reiterate your enthusiasm and interest in the job, and mention any relevant information that might not have been covered in the interview.

THANK-YOU LETTERS

○ Thank the person(s) for their time and interest

○ Reiterate your interest in the position

○ Add any relevant information that has not yet been discussed

SAMPLE THANK YOU LETTER

November 29, 19XX

Mr. John Doe
Executive Director
RESEARCH INSTITUTE OF AMERICA
123 State Street
Sacramento, CA 95647

Dear Mr. Doe:

Thank you for interviewing me for the position of Director of Special Events. I am excited about this position and your desire to coordinate special events with your public relations program.

Your current good use of special events as membership benefits could easily be tied into your marketing program. For example, I have found that if a direct mail membership campaign immediately follows a special event, there is a significantly higher response to the mail campaign. Community visibility can easily be increased with the proper selection of vendors for special events.

These are only two of the many effective techniques I have used successfully and would bring to your organization as Director of Special Events.

Thank you again for thinking of me. I would certainly enjoy being a part of your team.

Sincerely,

Sandra J. Beverly

LETTERS OF RECOMMENDATION

Letters of recommendation are used for job-hunting, educational programs, and some associations. An effective letter of recommendation will give the context for your association with the person, give specifics that support more general remarks that are made, and conclude with an overall statement of evaluation.

SAMPLE LETTER OF RECOMMENDATION

July 7, 19XX

Committee Chairman
THE COMMITTEE OF BAR EXAMINERS
OF THE STATE BAR OF CALIFORNIA
333 South Beaudry Avenue 10th Floor
Los Angeles, CA 90017

Reference: Thomas Glen Borst
           569110898-0913-23-00957

Dear Committee Chairman:

I highly recommend Thomas Borst as a candidate of exemplary moral integrity to pursue the profession of law. I have known Tom for approximately five years as a friend and colleague.

Tom and I have had many conversations about the practice of law and I have followed his coursework in obtaining a law degree with great interest. Tom is a hard-working individual, but more importantly, his motives for practicing law are more altruistic than perhaps most candidates you are considering.

I would feel very comfortable as a client of Tom's and feel he would do his best to represent me, treat me with a high degree of consideration, and charge me fairly for his services. I'm not sure I could say that of many of the approximately twenty-five lawyers I know or have worked with across the country.

Although I'm not sure our country needs more lawyers, if we are to have them they should be of Tom's moral fabric and ethical foundation.

Sincerely,

Robert B. Nelson

LETTERS OF RECOMMENDATION

○ Give relationship context

○ Specifics to support general
  remarks

○ Conclude with an overall evaluation

_____
_____
_____
_____
_____
_____
_____
_____

CHAPTER 10

Write It: Reference Material and Exercises

AVOIDING SEXIST LANGUAGE

To avoid unintentional sex discrimination, drop pronouns that specifically refer to either sex. Accepted ways of doing this include the following:

1. Rewrite the sentence to eliminate the need for the pronoun. For example:

    Avoid: The clerk certifies the correctness of her daily sales by putting her initials and the date on the tape.

    Preferred: The clerk certifies the correctness of the daily sales by initialing and dating the tape.

    Preferred: The clerk initials and dates the tape to certify the correctness of the daily sales.

2. Use a plural noun and they, their or them.

3. Repeat the noun.

4. Use "he or she" or "him or her." This is permissible, but can be awkward and should not be overused.

OVERUSED AND INEFFECTIVE PHRASES

The following phrases are overused in business writing and are generally meaningless and ineffective.

according to our records
acknowledge receipt of
acknowledge with pleasure
acknowledging yours of
advise (meaning to tell)
and oblige
answering yours of
anticipating your advice,
  favor, order, reply
as captioned above
as per
as regards
as stated above
assuring you of
as to your favor, esteemed
  favor
at all times
at an early date
at hand
at the present time
at the present writing
at this time
attached hereto, herewith
attached please find
awaiting your further
  wishes
awaiting your order, reply

beg to acknowledge,
  advise, assure, confirm

beg to call your
  attention to
beg (begging) to remain
beg to state, suggest

carefully noted
check to cover
complying with your
  favor of
complying with your
  request
concerning yours of
contents noted, duly
  noted
continued patronage

deem (for think)
desire to state
due to the fact
duly noted

enclosed find, please find
enclosed herewith
esteemed favor, order,
  request
even date

favor (for letter)
favor us with your reply
for your files
for your information

hand you herewith
has come to hand
have before us
have your kind favor
hereby advise, insist
herewith enclose, find,
    please find
hoping for your favor,
    order
hoping to receive

I am (ending
    last sentence)
I beg to advise
I have your letter of
I trust
in accordance with
in answer to same,
    to yours
in conclusion would state
in connection therewith
in due course
in re
in reference to
in receipt of
in reply to your favor
in reply would advise,
    wish
in response to yours, your
    favor
in the amount of
in the near future
in this connection
instant (inst.)

kind favor, indulgence,
    order

kindly advise, be advised
kindly confirm same

looking forward to

may we suggest
many we hope to receive
meets your approval

of above date
order has gone forward
our Mr. ___
our line
our records show

past favor
per
permit us to remind
please accept, advise, be
    advised
please find enclosed,
    herewith
please note
please rest assured
please return same
pleasure of a reply
proximo (prox.)
pursuant to

re
recent date
recent favor
referring to yours of
regarding the matter, the
    above
regarding said order
regarding yours
regret to advise, inform,
    state

replying to your favor of

said (the said regulation)
same (regarding same)
soliciting your advice,
 indulgence, patronage

take pleasure in
take the liberty of
thanking you in
 anticipation, advance
thanking you kindly
the writer
this is to acknowledge,
 advise
trusting we have
trusting to receive same

ultimo (ult.)
under separate cover
up to this writing

valued favor, order,
 patronage

we are pleased to advise,
 note
we have before us

we remain (ending last
 sentence)
we take pleasure in
 advising
we trust
wish to advise, state
with kindest regards
with reference to
with respect to your favor
with your kind
 permission
would advise, state
would wish to

your esteemed favor,
 order
your favor has come to
 hand
your future patronage
your kind indulgence
your letter of even date
your Mr. ___
your valued favor,
 patronage
yours of even date
yours of recent date
yours duly received

WORDY PHRASES AND PREFERRED REPLACEMENTS

Instead of using the wordy phrases in the left-hand column of the following list, try replacing them with the clearer, more concise versions in the right-hand column.

INSTEAD OF	TRY
Advisable that a study be made	Advisable to study
Afford an opportunity	Allow
At the present time, at this writing	Now
By means of	By
Come to a conclusion	Conclude
Created the possibility	Made possible
Despite the fact that	Although
Due to the fact that	Because
During the course of	During
During the time that	While
Experience has indicated that	Learned
For the reason that	Since, because
From the standpoint of	According to
Give consideration to	Consider
Goes under the name of	Is called
In a manner similar to	Like
In large measure	Largely
In the event that	If
In the near future	Soon
In the same way	Similarly
In spite of the fact that	Although
In view of the fact that	Since, because
Is indication of the fact that	Indicates that
Is in the process of correlation	Is being correlated
Is responsible for selecting	Selects
Is such as to negate the feasibility of	Precludes
It is recommended that consideration be given to	We recommend that
It is this that	This
It would thus appear that	Apparently
Leaving out of consideration	Disregarding

Make allowance for	Allow for
Make provisions for	Provide for
Most of the time	Usually
Numerals are used to identify	Numerals identify
Of the order of magnitude of	About
On the basis of	From, by, because
On the occasion of	When or on
Prior to	Before
Produce reduction in cost	Reduce cost
Referring to Figure 1-1 it will be noted that	Figure 1-1 shows
Resulting in death	Fatal
Serves the function of being	Is
Subsequent to	After
Takes appropriate measure	Acts, does
The computer in question	This computer
The fullest possible extent	The most
The greatest percent	Most
The treatment having been performed	After treatment
There can be little doubt that this is	This probably is
Throughout the entire area	Throughout
Throughout the whole of this experiment	Throughout this experiment
To make an approximation as to how much	To estimate, to approximate
Two equal halves	Halves
Undertake the removal of	Remove
With a view to	To
With due regard for	For
With reference to	About
Without making any noise	Noiselessly

EXERCISE: REWRITING PASSIVE SENTENCES

Rewrite each of the following passive sentences and phrases in an active voice, paying special attention to your verbs. Possible corrections follow.

1. Unsatisfactory results have been reduced through use of a new wash.

2. Designing of the pilot plant was carried out by two engineers.

3. Evaporation of the liquid takes place when . . .

4. Present designs are predicated upon the assumption that the material is homogeneous.

5. Solution of the salt is accomplished by application of heat.

6. The rayotube is dependent upon radiant energy for its application.

Suggested sentence rewrites:

1. A new wash reduced unsatisfactory results.

2. Two engineers designed the pilot plant.

3. Liquid evaporates when . . .

4. The designers assumed the material was homogeneous.

5. Heat dissolves the salt.

6. The rayotube needs radiant energy to operate.

EXERCISE: ACCENTUATING THE POSITIVE

Good business writing is positive and professional, even when the overall message is disappointing or negative. Following are sentences which are overly negative. Circle any "flag words" which are negative, then attempt to rephrase the sentences, replacing or eliminating the negative words. Make the sentences at least neutral or, if possible, positive — placing the "good news" first.

1. We cannot comply with your request for a catalog.

2. My letter explicitly stated my expectations; you obviously chose to ignore my wishes.

3. Your complaint about the damaged shipment will receive our careful attention.

4. We don't guarantee lost merchandise.

5. This corrects the negative balance in the amount of the check due us.

6. We regret to inform you the position has been filled.

7. Due to production problems, we cannot ship your order before October 1.

8. We simply don't understand your failure to pay this bill.

9. Until we see the specification, we cannot quote you a price.

10. In your letter, you claim we miscalculated the price.

11. You certainly should know we did not offer you any such concession.

12. We must point out that we shipped your order on June 20.

Possible sentence rewrites:

1. We'll be delighted to send you our latest catalog as soon as we receive them from our printer.

2. I am eager to move ahead—did you receive my recent letter?

3. Thank you for your recent information concerning shipment Number _____. We will give you whatever attention is necessary in order to satisfy your needs.

4. Please provide the details of your order so that we may trace shipment.

5. Thank you for your recent payment.

6. You seem very qualified for several positions. We will forward your resume on to managers that may have position openings that meet your qualifications in the near future.

7. We'll be glad to ship your order by October 1.

8. Please let us know if you have been billed incorrectly, otherwise we would appreciate prompt payment.

9. We'd be glad to quote you a price as soon as we have seen the specification.

10. Let us clarify how we determined the price . . .

11. To our knowledge, we did not offer you the concession you mentioned.

12. We shipped your order on June 20. Please let us know if you have not received it by June 23.

PART THREE

Refine It

CHAPTER 11

Edit

RULE 1: ELIMINATE UNNECESSARY WORDS

RULE 2: RELAX STUFFY LANGUAGE

RULE 3: SHORTEN YOUR SENTENCES

A woman attended a writing class of ours for hospital employees. When asked what she wanted to learn at the session, she replied, "To be able to turn out perfect copy the first time." Immediately, we smiled. She knew why. Rarely can any writer create perfect copy the first time.

Experienced writers know that good writing primarily comes from extensive *rewriting*. By mastering the steps in this book *you will turn out better copy the first time*. Still, this final step, "Refine It," will teach you how to move your letter from ordinary to outstanding. In this section, you will learn tools to polish and perfect your letter to make it meet your needs and be memorable for your reader.

Read your letter with these questions in mind:

○ Have I written to the audience that I want to address?

○ Did I address the topic from the reader's perspective?

○ Have I accomplished my original purpose in writing this letter?

○ Have I used the appropriate tone for the people or person who will receive it?

○ Is my language natural and comfortable?

○ Did I ask for what I want?

We will first discuss the importance of editing in which we focus on three crucial rules: eliminate unnecessary words, relax stuffy language, and shorten your sentences.

RULE 1: ELIMINATE UNNECESSARY WORDS

Many people think that writing better requires them to reformulate and restate entire phrases, sentences, and paragraphs. Again, in school we were taught to redo, rework, rephrase, restate. Longer was better. That's not the case at all! Often editing merely involves cutting out, not completely rewriting.

Cutting is like working with scissors. If you've written a phrase or sentence and you've gone back to revise it, there may be many extra words that you don't need. Take this example:

> *Poor:* There is no doubt but that we need to make changes in our company.

The sentence is grammatically acceptable, but wordy. "There is no doubt but that" is awkward and lengthy to digest. You could just as easily write,

> *Better:* Doubtless we need to make changes in our company.

or

> *Better:* We need to make changes in our company.

While we're on this subject, look at the first two words, "There is." "There is," "There are," "There was," and "There were," are called expletive constructions. Expletives are extras. These words begin wasted expressions that will not enhance or energize your composition. When you refine, get rid of these useless introductions. You want to begin with power. It's those first words that make the most memorable impression. Listen to one more sentence with wasted words:

Poor: He is a man who works for Crown Corporation.

"He is a man who"—which words could you cut? What about "is a man who"? Again, extra words. Just say,

Better: He works for Crown Corporation.

Those are the essential words in that sentence. No others need to stay.

Remember, your letter should state your message briefly. Extra words delay its impact and power. A sentence should contain only necessary words. "Is a man who" contains unnecessary words; delete them and you're on your way to a much more effective sentence. Another example:

Poor: In a hasty manner, I finished my work.

You could shorten the whole thing to say, "Hastily, I finished my work." "Hastily," is more visually compact and verbally powerful.

How about "the fact that you asked me makes me want to give my opinion." "The fact that" is an awkward construction. Lots of people start their sentences with "the fact that," yet none of those three words has any real charge.

How about another one: "This is a subject that interests me." Why not cut out the extra words? "This subject interests me" is a shorter, more powerful sentence than its predecessor.

Banks are making great changes today, but they are still, in many cases, holding onto archaic jargon that does not result in strong, clear writing. For instance, "A check was issued in the amount of $49.20" could be cut to "We issued a check for $49.20." It's more direct.

So cut out extras. They contribute nothing significant to the literary force of your sentence, and they delay the delivery of your message.

The senior trainer for a large bank assembled her new employees at their downtown branch for a demonstration on how to take customer deposits.

An elderly gentleman walked to the window with a complicated transaction. In her most long-winded "banking-ese" she told him how to fill out his slips and complete the transaction. He listened attentively but moments later, looked up at her and said, "I don't understand one word you just said."

Embarrassed, she realized her error. She cut her explanation in half, simplified her language, and got her point across much more successfully. Both she and her trainees learned a lot that day.

ELIMINATING REDUNDANCIES

Another category of words that delays or impedes clarity is unnecessary modifiers, also known as redundancies. These are phrases like:

○ "Loud explosion"

○ "High peak"

○ "Empty vacuum"

or that Madison Avenue favorite

○ "A most unique product"

CONDENSE WORDY PHRASES

Instead of:	Use:
call your attention to the fact that	remind you
an example of this is the fact that	for example
afford an opportunity	allow
due to the fact that	because
exhibit a tendency to	tend to
for the purpose of	for, to
in reference to	about, regarding
in view of the fact that	because
in the normal course of our procedure	normally
in the majority of circumstances	usually

(If it's "unique," it is one of a kind.) Redundant phrases feature repetition or excessive explanation, both utterly unnecessary in business writing. Numerous examples of unnecessary redundancies are found at the end of this section.

But what about repetition to reinforce an idea? Some people think that repeating certain statements gets the idea across more strongly. Repetition is no compliment to your reader's intellect, particularly in letters. If you said it clearly the first time, there's no need to go over it again. Repetition might be fine for an advertisement, but not for a letter. Spare yourself, and your audience; say it clearly and effectively one time only.

An excerpt from a repetitive letter:

> *Poor:* An additional statement will be added to the report.

If you know the statement will be added, you know it will be additional, right? Keep your sentences as short and as tight as you possibly can. By eliminating unnecessary repetition, you get right to the point and powerfully.

One more example:

> *Poor:* Notify the supervisors of any typing to be required between the hours of 4:00 and 6:00 p.m.

It's obvious that 4:00 and 6:00 are hours because they've got the "p.m." behind them. There's no need for "the hours of." Instead, write

> *Better:* Notify the supervisors between 4:00 and 6:00 p.m. of any typing you need.

or

> *Better:* Notify the supervisors of typing to be done
> between 4 and 6 p.m.

Tighten the sentence and you'll have taken off a lot of padding.

Instead of relating important information, many writers like to flaunt their egos in the beginning of their letters. Here's one who did exactly that:

> *Poor:* In my opinion, I think there is a good chance
> they will respond to our offer.

If you think it, it's evident that it's your opinion, and "in my opinion" is an egotistical and inefficient way to get going. Why not just begin:

> *Better:* I think they will respond to our offer.

Then you can support your opinion in the next part of the sentence.

> *Better:* I think they will respond to our offer to
> purchase two acres on the northeast corner of South
> Street. What do you think?

This last example includes only necessary information, says what you need to say, and puts your readers (rather than you) in the forefront. That's precisely what you want to do with your business writing.

DELETING UNNECESSARY PHRASES

Now let's talk about some specific phrases and ideas you want to leave out. Writers often rely on empty phrases to begin their sentences, that are meaningless, add nothing, and sap the vitality of much corporate writing. Avoid excessive explanations. You're writing a letter, not a lengthy proposal or a documented report, not a dictionary of terminology. Let the reader ask you if they have further questions, or want more text. However, in all our years of writing letters, we've never had anyone call us and ask, "Could you please write a longer letter the next time?"

PREPPING YOUR PREPOSITIONS.   This next sentence includes another grammatically interesting situation:

> *Fair:* A colleague of mine called yesterday.

The expression "of mine" is a prepositional phrase. Take that prepositional phrase and try this neat trick. Circle "of mine," change it into a one-word adjective and substitute it for "a colleague" so that the sentence reads,

> *Better:* My colleague called yesterday.

REDUNDANT REDUNDANCIES

at this point in time	personal physician
one a.m. in the morning	plan in advance
original founder	part and parcel
round in shape	two equal halves
consensus of opinion	black in color
close proximity	final conclusion
may possibly	refer back to
safe and sound	reason why
mutual cooperation	resume again
quite unique	right and proper
basic essentials	continue on
end result	necessary requisite

REDUNDANT PHRASES

Redundant	Preferred
Visible to the eye	Visible
Sufficient enough	Sufficient
Rectangular in shape	Rectangular
In the form of a square	Square
Red in color	Red
The month of December	December
Horizontal level	Level
First originated	Originated
Consensus of opinion	Consensus
My personal opinion	My opinion
Surrounded on all sides	Surrounded
Mesh together	Mesh
Combine together	Combine
Enclosed herewith	Enclosed
Attached hereto	Attached

See how that works?

If you're writing a letter to someone who's recently written you, you might start with the sentence,

Fair: A letter from you arrived on my desk yesterday.

Why not tighten it up to read,

Better: Your letter arrived yesterday.

It's an improvement for more than one reason. In addition to being simpler and more direct, it spotlights the reader instead of the writer. Everyone enjoys reading a letter with "you" or "your" rather than "I" or "my." It's a subtle way to win people over with your writing. Remember to adopt the "you" attitude.

Where can you cut the fat out of the following sentence?

> *Fair:* Below are provided general guidelines which should be followed for review purposes.

Often writers dilute the strength of their sentences by starting with empty words. They also try to tack on extra words at the end of the sentence. Does the word "purposes" mean anything much in the above sentence? Not really. Why not conclude with the word "review?" Lots of empty words like "purposes" fill people's writing. Just write:

> *Better:* Below are guidelines for review.

More examples and exercises about removing unnecessary words appear in Chapter 15.

CUT OUT CLICHES.   You can also cut out empty words and phrases by eliminating cliches. What exactly is a cliche? It's an overused, often outdated phrase that's lost any relevant meaning or impact. Common cliches from everyday communication include:

- "As far as the eye can see"
- "Blind as a bat"
- "Dead as a doornail"
- "It's old hat"
- "We don't see eye to eye"
- "That's the way the ball bounces"

○ "When in doubt, leave it out"

○ "Last but not least"

○ "In the final analysis"

○ "In the long run"

For instance, you may say in a letter, "It might be old hat to you, but let's review the company policy on tardiness." The trouble is that "it's old hat" isn't new, and it's not a clear way of speaking to your readers. Originality and personality are keys to effective business writing. When you use somebody else's business writing words, you aren't giving the best of yourself.

Rely on your own voice to phrase your words; they'll be a lot more "you"!

OVERDOING THE OBVIOUS.   Other phrases that can easily be cut out of your letters are phrases that overstate the obvious. Writers often begin their sentences by warming up like a baseball pitcher. In the process, they waste the words that are guaranteed to grab their reader's attention. Examples are phrases such as:

○ "as you know"

○ "that is to say"

○ "in other words"

○ "to repeat myself"

We advise you to avoid these altogether. If you've said something in certain words, or you've said it clearly, you don't need other words to say it again. Don't insult your readers' intelligence by telling them things they already know.

Cut out extras: words, phrases, ideas, and any information not absolutely essential to your letter's efficiency and effect. Use these guidelines to make your writing as efficient as possible.

OMIT UNNECESSARY WORDS

○ "Windup" words

○ Redundancies

○ Empty words, phrases

○ Cliches

○ Expletives

○ Repetition

RULE 2: RELAX STUFFY LANGUAGE

Relax your stuffy language and your letters will sound as if someone natural and congenial wrote them, instead of a pompous, pretentious person. To be easily understood, your language and word choice should be simple, not stuffy and contrived.

You can measure the complexity of your language through an analysis of your word choices, and the average length of your sentences in an activity called the "fog index," presented in Chapter 15.

Here's a short list of stuffy, longwinded phrases versus natural, straightforward words.

LONGWINDED	*VERSUS*	*STRAIGHTFORWARD*
In order to		To
Ten a.m. in the morning		Ten a.m.
In view of		Because or since
In the event of		If
Prior to		Before
With reference to		About (or omit)
With regard to		About (or omit)
Upon that date		On that date
At that point in time		Then
At this point in time		Now
Past experience		Experience

Would you say, "Prior to coming to work this morning, I made three phone calls"? If you did, I think your colleagues would stare at you—and probably with good reason. No, you'd say, "Before coming to work this morning . . ." You speak in a clear, conversational manner, why not write the same way? Look at some of the following sentences and see how they could be simplified.

> *Poor:* It is necessary that the material be received in this office by June 10th.

"It is" often begins lengthy, passive sentences, and "be received" is awkward as well.

> *Better:* We need the material by June 10.

or

> *Better:* The material must reach us by June 10.

You should also consistently focus on your reader's need, not your own. Most writing is self-centered, starting with pronouns "I" and "we." Why not highlight your reader instead of yourself, using more "you's" than "we's?"

> *Poor:* I would like to extend congratulations for a job well done.

> *Better:* Congratulations on the job you did.

or

> *Better:* Congratulations on your excellent work.

These sentences highlight the person who did the job, not your congratulations to them.

Read the way a group of readers was addressed:

> *Poor:* It is requested that all personnel planning to take leave in December fill in the enclosed schedule.

If you received this kind of letter, you'd probably feel very depersonalized and disregarded; I know I would. Why not write a letter that talks directly to your audience?

> *Better:* If you plan to take leave in December, please fill in the enclosed schedule.

RELY ON EVERYDAY WORDS.   The complexity of business and the need for precision do require some lengthy words, but don't use them when simple ones will do. People who speak in simple words often let lengthy ones burden their writing. For example, you might say, "help," but you write "assistance." You might say "pay" yet write "remuneration." These are inflated, overdressed words. Here are some more. Instead of saying "start," you write "commence," "help" becomes "facilitate," "best" turns to "optimum," "use" to "utilize." Some people call these words "businessese" or "corporatese." Whatever you call them, they don't work well in business writing.

Imagine it's 4 p.m. on a Thursday. You are busy, tired, and overworked. What's your response (visually, intellectually, and emotionally) to the next letter sample? Compare it to the improved letter that follows.

Mix your sentence length as you would when speaking to give variety and interest to what you have to say. If possible, limit your sentences to 20 words. There is an eye test for your sentence length; if it runs over three typed lines, it's probably too long. There's an ear test as well: read your writing out loud. If you have to breathe in the middle of a sentence you're probably boring (or inundating) your listeners with too much talk.

Look for opportunities to reach out to your reader. Ask more questions. Instead of saying,

> *Poor:* Please notify this department as to whether the conference has been rescheduled.

POOR LETTER SAMPLE

Subject: CUSTOMER SUGGESTIONS

Attached please find a Customer Suggestion Form which was sent to our area for review and comment. Based upon input from Legal, Mail Services, Item Processing, Credit Cards, and Investment Support, we feel that implementation of this suggestion would not be feasible at this time. The major concern regarding the suggestion came from the Legal Department. They felt that if this were implemented, it would have to be done on a selective basis by employees due to the possibility of exposing confidential information.

Complaints Department

IMPROVED LETTER SAMPLE

Subject: REPLY TO CUSTOMER SUGGESTION

Dear Valued Customer:

Thanks for submitting your suggestion! Our legal,
mail services, item processing, credit cards, and
investment support people thought it might not be
possible right now. The legal department felt that if
we used the suggestion it would have to be done
selectively. They're worried about exposing confidential information. However, we thank you for your
suggestion.

Sincerely,

Tim Zimsi
Customer Relations Representative

Why not just say,

Better: Has the conference been rescheduled?

Questions engage your readers' attention and interest and
bring them closer to you. Lazy writing overuses vague
terms and uses weak adjectives. Look at these phrases:
"Immense dedication," "enhanced programs," "viable
hardware." Such broad terms don't communicate specifics.
Just reading those terms, do you have any notion of what
they really mean? I don't think so. Use concrete examples
rather than abstract adjectives to communicate more effectively and efficiently to your reader.

WRITE TO EXPRESS, NOT TO IMPRESS.   People like to let
formal lingo creep into their writing, as if that gives them
more authority. Your signature should carry your authority, not your words. Instead of saying "aforesaid" and
"heretofore," "herewith is" and "notwithstanding," why

don't you more casually write "that," "until now," "here is," and "in spite of"? "The aforesaid information, herewith defines your legal rights," can be "That information tells you what legal rights you have."

The best writers impress their readers through language that doesn't call attention to itself. You don't want your readers to be distracted by the language itself; you want them to be moved by the content. It's like wearing a very fancy or distracting outfit; it calls attention to you but away from the subject that you're trying to present. There's nothing wrong with plain talk that gets your words across. Instead of saying "the undersigned," you can certainly refer to yourself as "I." Just don't overuse "I" in your writing.

Keep your writing as direct, concise, and precise as you can. Don't use a general word if the context calls for a specific one. Be as definite as you can. The best of writers know that the more specific an image their readers visualize, the better. For example, instead of "aircraft," say "plane." Instead of saying, "plane," say "DC-10." Instead of saying "improved costs," give them the exact amount.

Tell them in which direction you're going. "We have an enhanced method for producing your product" is vague. Is the method faster or cheaper? What about the method makes it better? What specifically is the improvement you're talking about? "Communication," someone once said, "is never having to say, 'huh' after you've read a letter." The more specific and concrete you are, the more you come across as an authoritative, responsible writer.

Your letters are the daily, most powerful way to create a positive image for yourself and your company. It's the least expensive, yet most effective way that you can project life and efficiency from you to all the people you need to communicate with on a regular basis. Removing the am-

---

RELAX STUFFY LANGUAGE

Poor: "We are in receipt of your recent letter concerning your account."

Better: "We received your recent letter about your account."

Poor: "We are endeavoring to minimize problems, where feasible.

Better: "We're trying to reduce problems, where possible."

Poor: "It is realized that you will have to effect numerous modifications."

Better: "We realize that you'll have to make many changes."

---

biguities saves time and money, and helps to create a positive, warm, and welcome image that no amount of advertising or budgeting can bring to you.

RULE 3: SHORTEN YOUR SENTENCES

If you wanted to lower your blood pressure, you'd need a baseline figure to work from. The same goes for sentence length. In order to cut down the length, you have to know how your sentences are running.

Look at the last letter you wrote. Count the number of words in an average sentence. What did you get?

- ○ 20?
- ○ 15?
- ○ 25?
- ○ 10?
- ○ 30?

If your sentences are consistently over twenty words, all one length, or all one style, you need to pay attention to these patterns and begin to change them. The strongest sentences are under twenty words, varied in length, and varied in style.

Most people never consider how many words they customarily use. It doesn't matter much, you may say. On the contrary, it could be of critical importance to your writing. Besides, if you are like most people you were trained in school that "longer is better" (from assignments where the total page length seemed paramount), so you use as many words as you can to round out your sentences and fill up your pages.

Psychologically, people don't like to read long sentences. Do you? Recall the most recent business letter you read that made an impact on you. It probably wasn't lengthy. It probably didn't fill up one page and spill over onto another page.

There's no golden rule to regulate how many words should be in a sentence. Research has shown that about 20 words is an average number for the reader to comprehend comfortably. If you go beyond, it's likely you're either repeating, adding redundant words or phrases, or splicing on a new idea. We recommend that you have an idea of how many words you write in an average sentence, then consciously try to limit your sentences to 16–20 words, at the most.

If you had to describe at this moment, verbally, what you do at your job, what would you say? You'd probably react to this request articulately and succinctly. You'd say, "I'm the department manager for my computer firm." Or, "I am a member of the nursing staff." Or, "I write news-letters for my company." That's very straightforward. And yet, if I were to ask you to transform the same body of information into writing, what would happen?

Probably the 10 to 12 words you spoke would suddenly swell to 20 or 25. Why? Individuals often admit that they expand their writing on paper to impress their readers with either their importance or their intelligence. Unfor-tunately, the outcome is often the opposite of what they intend. Wordiness distances you from your readers.

Monitor the number of words you write in your sen-tences from the start. See if you can keep them under control. To test for length, you can count the number of words and limit them. An average sentence should run no longer than a couple of lines on a typed page; this is another way to test effective sentence length. Less is fine. The *maximum* for business correspondence should be 30 words per sentence.

Another technique to check the length of your sen-tences is to read your sentence aloud. If you have to take a second breath before finishing, your sentence is too long. So, give your sentences the count, eyeball, or breath test. If they fail any of these, rewrite and shorten them.

Business writers also tend to use the same number of words in sentence after sentence. It's like listening to a speaker who has a monotone voice. It is boring to hear somebody whose pitch, rate, and volume never vary! Ev-eryone does it unconsciously, to some degree, in person and on paper. Monotony can creep into and deaden writ-ing the same way it does speaking. The antidote to this poison is simple: vary the number of words in your sentences. In fact, when you have a very important point to make, say it in a short sentence for greater impact and variety. Here's a monotonous letter opening:

> *Poor:* Please make sure you come back from your
> lunch break on schedule. The schedule of your hours
> is posted in the Staff Room. Please let me know if you
> have special plans.

It's boring because all the sentences read in a basic pattern and run the same length. Spice up your sentences this way.

> *Better:* Lunch schedules are important. Yours is
> posted in the Staff Room. It's important that you
> come back on time, but if you have special plans
> please clear them with me before you leave the office.

"Okay," you might say, "how do I shorten my sentences? It's all very well to say I know I need to shorten them. How can I make that happen?" The good news is that you don't have to do a whole rewrite. Just break or split your sentences.

SPLIT THE SENTENCE.   What does this mean? Tighten and shorten your sentences. Long sentences tend to be either two thoughts tacked together or one thought with

---

TIPS FOR SHORTER SENTENCES

○ Keep the average sentence length to 16
  words per sentence or less

○ Vary the length of your sentences

○ Use lists whenever you can

additional, unnecessary words. A sentence contains one primary thought. Yet some writers use a single sentence to jam two disjointed ideas together. So when you monitor your sentences, pay attention to this tendency. As a famous writer said, "Whenever you can shorten a sentence, do. And one always can. The best sentence? The shortest."

> *Poor:* In 1982, then corporate vice president Steven From, a dynamic speaker and organizer, established a new company, the Brown Organization, and persuaded a number of supervisors and managers to come to work for him.

This sentence is accurate, and it certainly contains necessary information. But it's quite long. Its flow is frequently interrupted. Where would you split it? You'll notice immediately that the natural breaking point is after the word "organization." Simply put a period after the word "organization," strike out the word "and," then add "he." You could also delete the words "a new company," since "established" indicates the company was new. What you have left is two shorter, tighter sentences closely linked, yet two units that are much more readable than the original.

Remember this guideline: look for the "and" and break before it. Frequently, people use the word "and" to say "chocolate and vanilla," connecting two items. That's fine. But it's not fine when you're connecting two major complete ideas to bridge one sentence to the next. Spot the "and" and break before it. Put a period before the "and," capitalize the first word in the next sentence, and then begin your new sentence. The result is two tight sentences instead of one loose, rambling one. The difference is startling.

> *Poor:* Every attempt was made to verify Mr. Smith's
> insurance, and I have attached for your information
> a written narrative of all the events that took place in
> our attempt to do this.

Again, there are two thoughts crammed into one lengthy unit. So, spot the "and" and break before it.

> *Better:* Every attempt was made to verify Mr. Smith's
> insurance. I have attached for your information a
> written narrative of all the events that took place in
> our attempt to do this.

Here you have two shorter, tighter sentences. You keep your reader engaged. Furthermore, you add variety in sentence length, which is desirable.

TAKE CARE WITH CONNECTIVES.   Writers unconsciously hook two ideas together with a connecting word instead of stopping the sentence, starting with an introductory connective, and continuing. The writer of the following letter wanted to pass the word to all members of his organization that he had been promoted.

> *Poor:* It is with mixed emotions that I leave the
> Eastgate facility; however, I am looking forward to
> my new endeavor with a great deal of enthusiasm
> and optimism, and you may be assured that I will do
> every thing possible to continue building the
> Eastgate facility.

That's a mouthful to say. In fact, it's also an eyeful for any reader.

What's your response to this writing? Probably to back off and remark, "Wow, I can barely get through that block of verbiage!" And that's how readers feel when they're confronted with writing that's consistently more than two lines of a typed page. It's too long.

For starters, examine the use of the word "however." This is a transition word or a connective: connectives are important. They show your reader that you're moving smoothly from one thought to the next. They also indicate relationships between ideas. In this case, the word is not necessary and could be eliminated. Alternately, it could begin a second sentence.

We often consult a list of connectives that help us keep our sentences from becoming too choppy or too broken up. When we need to glide smoothly from one thought into the next, we glance at the list to pick the correct connective. "However" is popular; others include "moreover," "nevertheless," and "consequently."

At the same time that we suggest you use connectives, we also want to warn you about them; some writers become so fascinated by them that they try to stick them into every single sentence, which is obviously too much. We also urge you to try to replace more formal connectives with informal ones, like "but," "so," and "now," especially in casual correspondence. The shift in today's business writing is from formal to informal. Your well-tuned ear will let you know when it's appropriate to follow.

If you're unfamiliar with connectives or transition words, begin to play around with them as a way to prevent your short sentences from becoming too choppy (a reservation writers often have when they're learning to limit their lengthy sentences). If you have a long sentence with a connective, one option is to end the sentence before the connective, then begin the new sentence with your connective. Here is an example:

Better: I'd like a new position. But, I've only worked here three months and don't have much experience.

Rather than one rambling, extended sentence, the writer now has two concise, smoothly connected sentences. The shift might not seem great, but read it both ways and listen to the difference. It is a more direct way of writing.

These are the top tools for shortening sentences. In turn, they will shorten your paragraphs.

○ Reduce the number of words.

○ Relax stuffy language.

○ Break up long sentences.

Use these guidelines to create positive, powerful responses in your reader's mind. Your writing will be stronger as a result.

CHAPTER **12**

Visuals: The Overall Look

WRITE WITH WHITE

USE LISTS TO CREATE
WHITE SPACE

USE HEADINGS TO CREATE
WHITE SPACE

BREAK UP LONG PARAGRAPHS

HIGHLIGHT YOUR KEY THOUGHTS

Look at your letter. Is it visually pleasing? Or is it a solid block of type? Are you drawn into your letter or are you pushed away? If you feel pushed away, so will your reader. To correct this reaction, break up your paragraphs; make them shorter and even more effective. There are a number of ways to create white space to rest your readers' eyes and give them some visual variety.

Look for visual guideposts. Have you divided your letter so that it reads effectively? Have you organized and segmented your writing in a clear way? Have you used subject lines? Have you indicated at the top of the letter to whom it goes and why? Have you used subparagraphs? If it is a lengthy letter, have you divided it up into subsections that will work effectively for your reader?

Create visuals through:

○ White space

○ Lists

○ Frequent paragraphs

○ Subject lines

○ Headings

WRITE WITH WHITE

When you first pick up a letter, what's your reaction? Too long? Too hard on the eye? No breaks? Writing is as much a visual as an auditory and intellectual experience. The way your words look on the page matters just as much as the way they sound when you read them. You might wonder, "What do looks have to do with this? Writing's nothing like fashion." But believe us, it is: When you see a piece of paper, your initial reaction is not to what you read, but what you see. It's like an initial meeting with someone. Sure, you're interested in what that individual has to say and what sort of person he or she is, but you're also impressed by what you see.

What is white space? When you look at a page, you see blocks of type broken by white space breaks. Just look at the sample letters in this chapter.

Let's face it: appearances are important. This applies to writing as well. The way your words look on a page has a great deal to do with whether they take your readers in or shut them out. You may ask, "What can I do to make my writing more visually appealing?" Exactly as you might ask an image consultant, "What can I do to make my physical appearance appealing?" (No, you don't want to write on day-glo paper with colored ink—that's not the type of attention you're after.)

Creating "white space" on the page is a subtle yet powerful method of producing a positive impression for your reader.

What does white space do? Something surprising—it rests your readers' eyes, invites them in, and motivates them to read over your letter thoroughly. Instead of over-whelming readers with a large block of type, you break up your letter into manageable chunks of material, giving them room to move along through what you've written, digesting it as they go.

NO WHITE SPACE

May 9, 19XX

Sales Associates
JBS Exclusives
1212 Eastern Ave.
Chicago, IL 60001

Subject: ERRORS & OMISSIONS

Your Errors & Omissions insurance contribution was
due February 28. Please give your $100 check to
Patty today or she will begin deductions from your
next commission check. We are waiting for the E&E
insurance quote from Mick S. Shires Company. As
soon as they answer, we will let you know.

Thanks!

Vicki Fuller
vf

cc: Leanne Wills
    James Zarro
    Caroline Bach
    Patty Le Wallen

WHITE SPACE

April 15, 19XX

John Brown
Sales Services Inc.
East Hartford Sq.
New York, NY 10003

Subject: EXPIRED LISTINGS

While examining my files, I ran across some expired listings. They are:

      2376-2388 Via Milla Street — expired April 1

      2393 Via Milla Street — expired February 3

Updated listings let you receive your commission checks. Please let me know *ASAP* about your status. If you have any current listings, let me know.

Thanks!

Mary Van Pelt
ml

cc: Jerry Fredd
    Suzi White
    Bill Bloomfield

USE LISTS TO CREATE WHITE SPACE

Creating white space by listing has been around for a long time and is sure to stay. Why? Because it's a great way to get your ideas on paper in an efficient, effective, and easy-to-read format.

Clear letters demand attention. So, when you write a letter, be aware of how it looks and reads. For example, you may have a complex sentence that's full of information. Maybe you've just come back from a meeting; you want to let your supervisors or subordinates know what you learned. Your initial inclination is to write a sentence something like this:

> *Poor:* The purpose of the workshop was to discuss state, local, and federal water quality regulations, the economic impact of waste control, and concepts and methods of monitoring wastes."

You've said precisely what the purpose of the meeting was, and you've expressed it with correct grammar and punctuation.

Look at that sentence a little more closely — what do you see? A block of type and a series of words stacked on top of each other. If we're extremely motivated, we'll muddle through, but it isn't inviting. You can write this same sentence more attractively without compromising its meaning. Set it up this way:

Better: The purpose of the workshop was to discuss:

    ○ Federal, state, and local water quality regulations

    ○ The economic impact of waste control

    ○ Concepts and methods of monitoring wastes

What do these changes accomplish? Everything! You've drawn attention to the three main subjects discussed at the workshop. Instead of burying them in an extended sentence, you've separated them so they stand out. By indenting the individual items, and placing bullets in front of them, you've used white space to put your reader's attention where you want it. We prefer to use a lower case "o" for bullets, although other symbols, such as "*" can also be used. Fill in the small "o"s so that they stand out more if you like. By using bullets, you catch your reader's eye and give your point more impact.

You may be wondering, "What about numbering my points?" In modern business writing, people often prefer bullets. Why? Because numbers, or letters, prioritize your points. Generally, listed items are often not written in a specific order of importance. If, however, you *do* want to designate priority to your list of items, by all means use numbers.

Look at the following example concerning goals for the new year:

Poor: Therefore, the following goals for 19XX to 19XX should accomplish these developmental needs of an effective marketing program. We want to establish a functional marketing framework, make a profitable, comprehensive profit and loss program, establish a customer satisfaction program, and develop an ongoing marketing audit of our share and growth program.

The grammar and punctuation are correct, but does the reader want to read it? No! You've lessened the impact of the paragraph. Listing your items gives them importance. Here's the same example using a list:

> *Better:* Therefore, the 19XX to 19XX goals should accomplish these developmental needs of an effective marketing program:
>
> ○ Establish a functional marketing framework
> ○ Develop a profitable, comprehensive program
> ○ Implement a customer satisfaction program
> ○ Create an ongoing marketing audit of our share and growth program

You put white space on the page to highlight your elements, make them important, and create readability.

ROUNDING OUT YOUR LISTS.   Now you know the basics of how to list your items. Can you think of a letter you wrote recently at work, one in which you didn't insert a list, but wish you had? Most readers and writers who discover this technique immediately use it as a most effective, efficient, and powerful way of developing and enhancing their writing skills.

Nevertheless, a client once called to say, "That's a terrific technique you taught my employees. The trouble with it is that now they want to list anything and everything!" A little caution: certainly, listing is powerful and effective, but as with your transitions, don't overdo it. If you list every single item in your letter, you may wind up with a laundry list instead of well-written material.

One final footnote to lists: instead of ending your paragraph with the last listed item, you can round it out with a sentence that will summarize the significance of the list itself.

Reexamine the following example, which was presented earlier:

The purpose of the workshop was to discuss:

- ○ Federal, state, and local water quality regulations
- ○ The economic impact of waste control
- ○ Concepts and methods of monitoring wastes

Instead of plunging into the next paragraph, try writing a summary sentence to follow the list. For example, you might say, "The workshop attendees felt the topic coverage was comprehensive."

That way you have sandwiched your list between one opening and one closing sentence, set off the items you want to list, and created a very visually appealing look on the page. Now you're ready to go into your next paragraph.

USE HEADINGS TO CREATE WHITE SPACE

There are several other ways to create white space on the page, and we urge you to consider them when you write.

Notice the way this book is set up. You have frequent breaks in each chapter. We've done that with subheads. They're a useful way to break up material, leading your reader from one topic to the next without breaking the continuity. Subheads create white space on the page. Each time you break a section, you have white space before your subhead, then the subhead itself, followed by the next section. That's called using "headers." More and more letter writers use them, and so can you! Here's an example of headers:

LETTER WITH HEADINGS

May 22, 19XX

Lois Gartella

Subject: NEW BIDS FOR THE WAREHOUSE ROOF

Patching Roof

Four roofers have submitted bids to repair the warehouse roof. The lowest bidder suggests patching rather than redoing the entire roof.

Repairing Roof

Others disagree with this bidder. They point out that the roof has already been patched too many times. It needs to be overhauled and have heat sealed polymer sheets applied.

Decision

I agree with the other bidders. Polymer roofing comes with a 20-year guarantee compared to 2 years. Since we desperately need a warehouse, I suggest we give the contract to the lowest bidder of the polymer system.

Meetings

Let's have a meeting next Tuesday at 3:15 p.m. in the lounge to discuss this decision.

Thanks!

Mike Foley

BREAK UP LONG PARAGRAPHS

There's nothing more distancing to your reader than writing one long paragraph after another. A solid block of type is hard on the eyes and the senses. Consequently, just as we've encouraged you to decrease your sentence length, we encourage you to decrease your paragraph length as well.

How many sentences per paragraph? Again, there's no golden rule. An average of seven to eight lines or 75 words per paragraph should suffice for most business correspondence. And back to what your teachers taught: the purpose of a paragraph is to present one idea and one idea only. So write your paragraph topic sentence, go into a brief explanation—possibly an example—then stop, move into your next paragraph with a transition or subhead, and you're on your way.

HIGHLIGHT YOUR KEY THOUGHTS

Finally, have you highlighted key ideas and indicated their relationships? You can do this using lists, subheads, parallel phrasing, and underlined ideas. As you read through your letter, try to imagine that you're the reader, not the writer. After all, it's the reader you're trying to reach, not yourself. How will they respond? What will they think of your writing? Will they be moved to action? Will they understand exactly what you're talking about, exactly what you want?

Write your letter and imagine your name is after "Dear," not "Sincerely." How does the letter read now? Is it persuasive, offensive, clear, or confusing? These vital questions will give you the essential feedback.

Test market your letter before you send it out. Either test it on somebody else in your company or imagine that you are the test market yourself. Does it read well? Does it look well? Will it move your reader to action? If all these requirements have been satisfied, then you have written a letter that speaks well for you.

The next letter was written by a hospital administrator. Would you have sent it? What recommendations would you make? Read it carefully, with your own guidelines in mind. Then look at our suggested revision.

The second letter is easier to read, it's more appealing to the eye, it has better organization, and it yells out, "Read me, read me!"

You realize that these letters are longer than usual. Also notice that your attention wandered, you wanted to skip on to new material, and you didn't really pay attention to the text. Well, the same goes for your letters. There's no absolute rule about maximum length of a letter. However, the letters that are longer than one page get skimmed rather than read. Letters can and should be more than one page only if the reader has asked for details that require a longer response.

A Baltimore businessperson once admitted to us that he gives himself thirty seconds to read a letter regardless of the length. If it's two pages he gives it thirty seconds; if it's half a page, thirty seconds. Needless to say, the shorter one gets read much more thoroughly.

So keep that in mind when you write your letters. Pace them like the best 30-second commercial you've ever watched.

LONG, DENSE LETTER

March 2, 19XX

Sam Green
Vice President
Administration
XYZ Corporation
New York, NY 10003

Subject: Multicompany Quality Assurance Committee Meeting of
          January 11, 19XX

I attended the first meeting of the 19XX Multi-Company Quality Assurance Committee today! A statement was made by Dr. Brown that for the last two years he served as Peer Review Committee Chairman and prior to that on the Audit Committee for Internal Medicine and they never had any direction or idea of what needed to be done. This came up because Dr. Adams states to all of the committee members that QA items must be on all agendas.

My concern is that Dr. Hunson is responsible for QA and Audit and Peer Review Committee meetings and should be attending these meetings and *providing that direction*. I believe it is written into his job description. Perhaps he has been sending only the QA Coordinator to the meetings and she really only pulls charts and does minutes and helps with the coordination of the activities. Dr. Hunson must provide the direction, and especially this year when we have more new chairpeople. I would like to suggest that Dr. Hunson's job description be reviewed and revised and I would like to suggest that this subject be discussed with Dr. Smith, Chairman of Quality Assurance. I would also like to suggest that Dr. Hunson be asked to attend every Department Specialty Meeting and discuss what types of Quality Assurance items should be addressed, how the topics should be picked, and how his department will assist the committees/departments in carrying out these assigned responsibilities.

I sincerely appreciate your consideration of my request. I see this as a major issue that should be taken care of immediately. I would like to see the new 1985 Committees provided with *direction* and *appropriate assistance* from Dr. Hunson.

Sincerely,

Joan Williams
Assistant Administrator

REVISED, IMPROVED LETTER

February 1, 19XX

Sam Green
Vice President
Administration
XYZ Corporation
New York, NY 10003

Subject: Responsibility of Multi-Company Quality
Assurance Committee

Dear Sam:

I have several recommendations as a result of my
attendance at the first Multi-Company Quality Assurance Committee meeting of 1987:

○ I recommend that Dr. Hunson, whose responsibilities include the QA, Peer Review,
   and Audit Committees, should attend all
   their meetings, providing direction and
   assistance.

○ I also recommend that Dr. Hunson be asked
   to attend all department specialty meetings
   to discuss what types of QA items should be
   addressed, how the topics should be chosen,
   and how his department can help the
   committees/departments carry out their QA
   assignments.

○ Finally, I feel that Dr. Hunson's job description should be reviewed and revised to clarify
   any confusion that may exist concerning his
   exact responsibilities in connection with
   these important committees.

I consider QA a major issue that should be given
immediate attention. I sincerely appreciate your
attention to my recommendations.

Sincerely,

Joan Williams
Assistant Administrator

CHAPTER 13

Proofread

MAKING THE FINAL INSPECTION

THE PROOF IS IN YOUR READING

FINAL RETOUCHES

When you feel you're finished writing, it means you have one last step: to proofread your work once again! Although you might be eager to move on to other work, we strongly believe that most mistakes in business writing are the result of not taking a few last minutes to double-check your work.

MAKING THE FINAL INSPECTION

Your letter sits in front of you. It must go out shortly. You probably want to proofread and send it right now. Don't! Put it away for as long as you can before you give it a final reread.

It's very hard to be an objective critic of your own writing. Hopefully, you like yourself enough to have an ego that doesn't want to criticize or be too hard on what you've written. Most people look at what they've just written and say, "That's pretty good." And so they send out copy with errors that might not appear to them, but will be apparent to someone else. Or, they look and say "this is awful!" and tear it up! So, after you've written, put your letter away from one to twenty-four hours. Then come back to it fresh.

Pretend that someone else has written your letter. Then critique it with an objective eye.

For your final proofreading you want to make sure that you have adhered to the objectives you established when you first began to write and the guidelines discussed in this book.

With these guidelines in mind, you can become an objective critic of your letter. Now, go through your writing quickly. See how the entire letter reads. Try reading it out loud. After all, how it sounds is how it's going to read. Reading your letter out loud will help you pick up language that doesn't work, pompous words, and phrases that are literary rather than conversational.

THE PROOF IS IN YOUR READING

Here are several other proofreading techniques:

○ If you want to get true distance from something you've written, run your letter through a copy machine. Then critique it as though someone else has written it. Most people are better editors than they are writers. This technique lets you play editor.

○ Try rereading your letter in a different light or a different room than where you've originally written it. This gives you additional distance and objectivity.

○ Read your letter into a tape recorder. In listening to it, you will hear it with added objectivity. "No," you might say, "that sounds like an awkward phrase," or, "I've got too many words in that sentence," or "that sentence just doesn't sound right." Again, hearing it gives you a greater, deeper, and more profound experience of exactly how this letter will work in the ears and eyes of your prospective reader. A recent convenience store client with a longstanding spelling problem told us that reading his letter aloud let him catch spelling mistakes he would have overlooked.

○ Read your letter backwards! That might sound like a gimmick, but if you read it backwards and move your eye across the page from right to left, you will be thrown out of your normal way of relating to your words and phrases. You'll notice spelling errors, repeated words, and punctuation mistakes that you wouldn't find in the ordinary course of rereading. Many people are so accustomed or bored with reading what they just wrote that their eyes automatically skip over glaring typographical errors. However, if you're reading it backwards, you will see problems you might not otherwise spot.

○ One of the best learning and critiquing methods is to find colleagues in your office to read your letters. You can do the same for them. That way you give each other ideas and feedback on your writing. It's another way of deepening a relationship in your company and finding out that other people struggle with the same writing issues that you do.

> People are initially hesitant to do this out of
> privacy, modesty, or not really wanting to
> share their writing difficulties with others.
> But after they've done it once or twice they
> find it a profitable and enjoyable experience.
> Also, they get clear feedback on their
> writing—the kind that they always wanted in
> school, but perhaps never really received.
> Instead of receiving a paper blighted with
> red marks, they hear constructive criticism
> and helpful ideas. A second party can pick up
> errors in organization, proofreading, and
> grammar that you might not spot yourself.

Those are some technical ways of reviewing your letter to ensure that what you have in the final draft is a far stronger product. You can make up your own set of guidelines for a final inspection. We'll give you a few and you can add to them your specifications and needs. It's like assembling a car. Before it leaves the assembly line, the inspectors look it over with quality-assurance guidelines in mind. They don't let that car leave the plant until it has passed maximum safety and product specifications. Well, the same care should be give to your letter!

FINAL RETOUCHES

Any rough draft you refine once or twice improves each time. So if you have done all the preliminary work, why not spend the time on refining? It's like getting dressed and putting the finishing touches on yourself. After all, you wouldn't go to an interview in a new, well-pressed suit and a big stain on your tie.

Many people commit the same type of error in writing. They spend a lot of time on the initial draft; it looks fine; they type it on the best stationery; and its format and message are worthy of attention and promotion. Yet in the final stages, they have a spelling error, a misplaced comma, or a grammatical mistake that undermines the authority, authenticity, and clarity of their letter.

A client recently told us of receiving an important letter spotted with coffee and the writer's lunch! The topic was appetizing; the messy look was not! Also beware of erasures, and other signs of hasty and hassled "final touches."

PROOFREADING TECHNIQUES

○ Let it sit

○ Read it aloud

○ Exchange with colleague

○ Read it backwards

○ Check reference materials

○ Make it perfect!

CHAPTER 14

Putting It All Together: An Example

Once you have a draft of your business letter, the final step is to review what you have written. First let's review some of the things we want to look for in our drafted letter:

- O Ask yourself these questions:
  - o Is my purpose clearly stated?
  - o Have I addressed my intended audience?
  - o Do I tell my readers what I want them to do?

- O Write the way you speak—naturally, as in day-to-day conversation.

- O Simple is strong. Where possible, substitute short and everyday language.

- O Use strong action verbs. Avoid "to be" verbs.

- O Use active voice.

- O If you must use passive voice, use it consciously and selectively. Use it for emphasis or when you purposely intend to be vague.

○ Avoid needless words and unnecessary jargon.

○ Write with short sentences and paragraphs.

○ Use smooth transitions between paragraphs.

○ Use lists and headings.

○ Proofread your letter.

With these points in mind, let's review the sample letter (p. 230) that one of our clients brought to us for help.

It's hard to tell what Barbara wants from Marshall Hall in this letter. Barbara told us she and her secretary spent several hours on this letter, rewriting, editing, and proofreading.

Here are some of our critiques of this letter:

○ Barbara buries the purpose of the letter, which concerns invoices and warranty numbers, in the second paragraph.

○ Unnecessary information clutters the letter. She presents facts San Diego Construction doesn't need to know.

○ It's too long; the wordiness and jargon can be cut.

○ The tone is too formal, and it patronizes the reader. The phrases "Mr. Joseph Kychik" and "your people" exemplify this patronizing tone.

○ She should list the main points, using headers or bullets.

April 14, 19XX

Mr. Marshall Hall
San Diego Construction Co.
5849 Ocean Way
San Diego, California 92101

Subject: FIRST OCEAN WAY—JOB #8500

Dear Marshall:

I am writing to thank you and the people of San Diego Construction Co.,
including especially Mr. Philip Hardy, for your role in helping to make First
Ocean Way a successful condominium project.

Now that the construction phase of the project is completed, I would like to
rearrange the business relationship between our companies. The ABC Company would like to look to San Diego Construction for help in two areas: (1)
making modifications for the operating division, and (2) performing warranty
work for the construction division. I am asking that before performing work,
your people determine which division is to receive and pay the invoice. Mr.
Joseph Kychik of the Operating Division can be reached at telephone number
619-555-5000. He can explain how invoices should be sent to the Operating
Division. Invoices for construction warranty work can be sent to the ABC
Company P.O. Box as they presently are.

In order to institute a measure of control over warranty expenses, I am
requesting that San Diego Construction obtain a warranty work order number
from Mr. Kychik before performing warranty work. He will obtain the number
from my office.

I have advised our construction accounting department to return any invoices
received for work performed on or after April 13, 19XX unless the warranty
work order numbers appear on the face of the invoice. Additionally, each time
sheet, equipment sheet, and material invoice must contain the warranty work
order number of which it applies. This is a little different from your present
system which describes the work done in words alone.

I will certainly appreciate the attention that you, Phil Hardy, and Sheila
O'Neal can give to make this system work. I am sure it will help us process
your invoices faster, since the need to decipher what was done and which
division is responsible for it will be eliminated.

Sincerely,

Barbara A. Francis
Project Manager
ABC COMPANY
JAL/jss

cc: P. Hardy
    J. Kychik
    S. O'Neal
    J. White
    J. Forbes

○ What does Barbara want Marshall Hall to do? She states the result, but the desired action is unclear.

○ She tries to write the letter to more than one person. She should send each person a separate letter.

Now, let's take a closer look at this letter.

PURPOSE.   Barbara muddies the purpose. Is she thanking San Diego Construction, or is she asking them to send their invoices to the proper division? Or does she want them to obtain warranty numbers and attach them to their invoices? The purpose should be stated clearly in the beginning of the letter. Use the inverted pyramid style. Always put your purpose or reason for the letter first, add in the facts later.

AUDIENCE. The audience is Marshall Hall. Barbara makes a mistake to also thank Phil Hardy and address Sheila O'Neal in this letter. She should send separate letters to Phil and Sheila. It is more polite and courteous. But just to send copies to these people isn't enough. Everyone appreciates a personal thank you. How would you feel if you received a xeroxed thank-you note?

TONE.   The tone is too formal. It almost insults the reader. We know Barbara means to be polite, but look at the phrases "the people of San Diego Construction," "Mr. Phillip Hardy," "Mr. Joseph Kychik," and "your people." She should say "your company," "Philip Hardy," "Joseph Kychik," and "you." It's friendlier and promotes a more helpful attitude.

ACTION. Barbara wants San Diego Construction to change its invoicing methods to get paid faster. But what *exactly* does Barbara want Marshall to do? This part is unclear.

We asked Barbara to look at the prewriting techniques and freewrite a new letter. Read her freewriting sample on page 233. Notice how she lets her mind wander. That's part of the freewriting technique.

Barbara enjoyed her freewriting. It unleashed her mind; her ideas flowed. Now let's examine the final rewrite (p. 234). Notice the changes in the format.

Notice how she stated the purpose in the beginning of the letter. She also shortened the sentences and paragraphs, then listed the procedures for Marshall to follow. The letter is now clearer, easy-to-read, and to the point. Will Marshall respond positively to Barbara's request? In all likelihood, yes—especially if he wants his money faster!

You're now nearing the end of *The Perfect Letter* and you're ready to write on your own. You can use the skills we've discussed in this book with any kind of writing— from memos, to letters, to longer proposals—and know that you are writing creativity, correctly, and concisely. You should now have the competence to be an excellent writer, and in time you will build confidence in your ability.

If you put what you have learned into practice, people will look forward to reading what you have written. They will welcome a letter from you and will, in all likelihood, act on it promptly. They'll praise you for your well-written letters and, hopefully, send you a perfect letter in return.

April 14, 19XX

Mr. Marshall Hall
San Diego Construction Co., Inc.
5849 Ocean Way
San Diego, California 92101

Reference: Job #8500

Subject: FIRST OCEAN WAY

Dear Marshall:

Now why am I writing? Oh, yes, to get you to change the way you bill us so we can pay you on time. Now how do I say that clearly. Let's see, I'm supposed to focus on just a few rules of business writing such as be conversational, use shorter sentences, and avoid cliches, and jargon. Ok, here goes . . .

I want to rearrange the business relationship between our companies. The ABC Company would like to look to San Diego Construction for help in two areas: Let's see, it might help to use bullets here.

○ Making modifications for the operating division

○ Performing warranty work for the construction division

Before sending your invoices, indicate, determine which of the ABC Company is to receive and pay the invoice. Joseph Kychik of the Operating Division, 619-555-5000, can tell you how Operating Division invoices should be sent. This should be a new paragraph I think. Maybe it can be deleted. OK, let's do it.

Construction warranty invoices will continue to go to the ABC Company P.O. Box. Well, maybe I didn't delete it, but I rewrote it instead. Please obtain a work order number from Joseph Kychik of the Operating Division before you begin any warranty work.

I have advised our construction accounting department to return any invoices received for work performed on or after April 13, 19XX unless the warranty work order numbers appear on the face of the invoice. Additionally, each time sheet, equipment sheet, and material invoice must contain the warranty work order number for which it applies.

Thanks for all your help in making our new system work. We are looking forward to working with you in the near future. How's that? I cut that last paragraph!

Sincerely,

Barbara A. Francis
Project Manager
ABC COMPANY
JAL/jss

cc: P. Hardy
    J. Kychik
    S. O'Neal
    H. White
    J. Forbes

April 14, 19XX

Mr. Marshall Hall
Vice President, Operations
San Diego Construction Co., Inc.
5849 Ocean Way
San Diego, CA 92101

Reference: Job #8500

SUBJECT: Changes in Our Invoicing Procedures

Dear Marshall:

Thanks for making the First Ocean Way Condominium project the success that it was. So that you can receive payments on time, we have decided to change our billing procedures. The benefits will outweigh any preliminary inconveniences.

Let me briefly list the new procedures that will affect San Diego Construction:

- Send all invoices to the proper ABC Division
- Continue to send construction warranty invoices to the ABC Company P.O. Box.
- Obtain a work order number from Joseph Kychik (619) 555-5000 before you begin any warranty work.
- List warranty work order numbers on time sheets, equipment sheets, and material invoices.

Our accounting department informed me today that it will return any invoices received for work performed on or after April 13, 19XX, unless the warranty work order numbers appear on the face of the invoice.

Thanks for your help in making our new system work. Proper use of the system will prompt quick payment.

I look forward to working with you again in the near future.

Sincerely,

Barbara A. Francis
Project Manager
ABC COMPANY

JAL/jss

cc: M. Floyd
    J. Forbes
    P. Hardy
    J. Kychik
    C. Miller

CHAPTER 15

Refine It: Reference Materials and Exercises

THE FOG INDEX

One measure of readability is the "fog index."* To determine your fog index complete the following steps:

1. Count off a 100-word writing sample.
2. Determine the average number of words per sentence.
3. Count the number of polysyllables.
4. Add (2) and (3).
5. Multiple by 0.4.

The resulting number is your fog index. For example:

Words per sentence	20
Polysyllables	<u>10</u>
add the two	30
multiply by	<u>.4</u>
Fog Index equals	12.0

---

*See Robert Gunning, *The Technique of Clear Writing* (New York: McGraw-Hill, rev. 1968), and Rudolph Flesch, *The Art of Readable Writing* (New York: Harper & Row, 1974).

The fog index gives an estimate of the number of years of education needed to read your writing. Since you want your writing to be easily understood, a low fog index is desirable—say, in the 6–7 range. This is where most best-selling books (including the Bible), magazines, and newspapers fall. A higher fog index (12–17) means your writing is more complex than needed to be understood. Typically, individuals who work in technical jobs such as engineering or computer science will write like this. The *Wall Street Journal*, *Atlantic Monthly*, and *New Yorker*, as well as most technical journals, fall in this range.

A lower fog index (4–5) is less frequently a problem with business writers. But though this writing would be simple and easy to understand, it is often choppy and therefore less readable.

Match your fog index to *your* audience! If your readers are mostly blue-collar workers, your fog index should be 5–7; high school graduates, 8–10; and college graduates, 11–13.

To alter your fog index, just focus on the two variables that were used in measuring it: word complexity and sentence length. Whenever possible choose the simpler, more conversational word when you write. Likewise, break up your sentences into shorter, more understandable thoughts.

On the following pages are additional simpler words and phrases to use in your writing.

SIMPLER WORDS AND PHRASES

INSTEAD OF	*TRY*
accompany	go with
accomplish	carry out, do
accorded	given
accordingly	so
accrue	add, gain
accurate	correct, exact, right
additional	added, more, other
address	discuss
addressees	you
addressees are requested	(omit), please
adjacent to	next to
advantageous	helpful
adversely impact on	hurt, set back
advise	recommend, tell
afford an opportunity	allow, let
aircraft	plane
allocate	divide, give
anticipate	expect
a number of	some
apparent	clear, plain
appreciable	many
appropriate	(omit) proper, right
approximately	about
as a means of	to
ascertain	find out, learn
as prescribed by	in, under
assist, assistance	aid, help
attain	meet
attempt	try
at the present time	at present, now
benefit	help
by means of	by, with

INSTEAD OF	*TRY*
capability	ability, can
close proximity	near
combat environment	combat
combined	joint
commence	begin
comply with	follow
component	part
comprise	form, include, make up
concerning	about, on
consequently	so
consolidate	combine, join, merge
constitutes	is, forms, makes up
contains	has
convene	meet
currently	now
deem	believe, consider, think
delete	cut, drop
demonstrate	prove, show
depart	leave
designate	appoint, choose, name
desire	want, wish
determine	decide, figure, find
disclose	show
discontinue	drop, stop
disseminate	give, issue, pass, send
due to the fact that	due to, since
during the period	during
effect modifications	make changes
elect	choose, pick
eliminate	cut, drop, end
employ	use
encounter	meet

SIMPLER WORDS AND PHRASES (cont.)

INSTEAD OF	TRY
endeavor	try
enumerate	count
equipments	equipment
equitable	fair
equivalent	equal
establish	set up, prove, show
evidenced	showed
evident	clear
exhibit	show
expedite	hasten, speed up
expeditious	fast, quick
expend	spend
expertise	ability, skill
expiration	end
facilitate	ease, help
failed to	didn't
feasible	can be done
females	women
finalize	complete, finish
for a period of	for
for example, _____ etc.	for example, such as
forfeit	give up, lose
for the purpose of	for, to
forward	send
frequently	often
function	act, role, work
furnish	give, send
has a requirement for	needs
herein	here
heretofore	until now
herewith	below, here
however	but

INSTEAD OF	TRY
identical	same
identify	find, name, show
impacted	affected, changed
implement	carry out, start
in accordance with	by, following, per, under
in addition	also, besides, too
in an effort to	to
inasmuch as	since
in a timely manner	on time, promptly
inception	start
indicate	show, write down
indication	sign
inform	tell
initial	first
initiate	start
in lieu of	instead of
in order that	for, so
in order to	to
in regard to	about, concerning, on
interface with	meet, work with
interpose no objection	don't object
in the amount of	for
in the event that	if
in the near future	shortly, soon
in view of	since
in view of the above	so
is applicable to	applies to
is authorized to	may
is in consonance with	agrees with, follows
is responsible for	handles
it appears	seems
it is essential	must, need to
it is requested	please, we request, I request

SIMPLER WORDS AND PHRASES (cont.)

INSTEAD OF	TRY
limitations	limits
limited number	few
magnitude	size
maintain	keep, support
majority of	most
maximum	greatest, largest, most
methodology	method
minimize	decrease, lessen, reduce
minimum	least, smallest
modify	change
monitor	check, watch
necessitate	cause, need
notify	let know, tell
not later than 10 May	by 10 May, before 11 May
not later than 1600	by 1600
notwithstanding	in spite of, still
numerous	many
objective	aim, goal
obligate	bind, compel
observe	see
operate	run, use, work
optimum	best, greatest, most
option	choice, way
parameters	limits
participate	take part
perform	do
permit	let
pertaining to	about, of, on
point in time	point, time
portion	part

INSTEAD OF	TRY
possess	have, own
practicable	practical
preclude	prevent
previously	before
prioritize	rank
prior to	before
proceed	do, go ahead, try
procure	buy, get
proficiency	skill
provide	give, offer, say
provided that	if
provides guidance for	guides
purchase	buy
pursuant to	by, following, per, under
reflect	say, show
regarding	about, of, on
relative to	about, on
relocate	move
remain	stay
remainder	rest
remuneration	pay, payment
render	give, make
represents	is
request	ask
require	must, need
requirement	need
reside	live
retain	keep
said, some, such	the, this, that
selection	choice
set forth in	in
similar to	like
solicit	ask for, request

SIMPLER WORDS AND PHRASES (cont.)

INSTEAD OF	TRY
state-of-the-art	latest
subject	the, this, your
submit	give, send
subsequent	later, next
subsequently	after, later, then
substantial	large, much
successfully complete	complete, pass
sufficient	enough
task	ask
terminate	end, stop
there are	exist
therefore	so
therein	there
there is	exists
thereof	its, their
the undersigned	I
timely	prompt
time period	time, period
transmit	send
under the provisions of	under
until such time as	until
validate	confirm
viable	practical
vice	instead of, versus
warrant	call for, permit
whereas	because, since
with reference to	about
with the exception of	except for
witnessed	saw
your office	your

AVOIDING REDUNDANCIES

Remove all unnecessary words from the following expressions:

under absolutely no
    circumstances
lift it up
in a dying condition
completely finished
first of all
a free gift
he continued on
a near facsimile
his final conclusion
on Easter Sunday
a complete monopoly
the actual truth
raise up the flag
he personally believes
she definitely decided
caught a tuna fish
sent none at all
it seemed to be
was finally settled
June sales to level off
a true fact
two complimentary passes
30 invited guests
was short in length

unasking, without question,
    he followed the order
in close proximity
finishing up soon
his advance predictions
was positively dangerous
was definitely identified
appeared to be ill
cost the sum of $10
broke an existing rule
for a short space of time
during the summer months
offered definite proof
made advance reservations
a frame made of iron
its final completion
a personal friend
the proven facts
consensus of opinion
will start off soon
her past experiences
a clever new innovation
its future prospects
will repeat again
whether or not

our hopeful optimism held
a bald-headed man
returned back home
set a new record
throughout the entire day
cannot possibly be
assembled crowd of people
his other alternative

a temporary recess
null and void
drop down abruptly
in the meantime
it first began
a noon luncheon
in court litigation

ANSWERS:

under no circumstances
lift it
dying
finished
first
a gift
he continued
a facsimile
his conclusion
on Easter
a monopoly
the truth
raise the flag
he believes
she decided
caught a tuna
sent none
it seemed
was settled
June sales to level
a fact
two passes
30 guests
unasking, he followed
   the order

in proximity
finishing soon
his predictions
was dangerous
was identified
appeared ill
cost $10
broke a rule
for a short time
during the summer
offered proof
made reservations
a frame of iron
   (or an iron frame)
its completion
a friend
the facts
consensus
will start soon
her experiences
a clever innovation
its prospects
will repeat
was short
whether

our optimism
a bald man
returned home
set a record
throughout the day
cannot be
assembled crowd
his alternative

held a recess
null *or* void
drop abruptly
meantime
it began
a luncheon
in court *or*
    in litigation

CONDENSING PHRASES

Compress the following statements into one word:

_____   the sum amount due

_____   as soon as possible

_____   at that time

_____   under no circumstances

_____   on one occasion

_____   whenever possible

_____   a small number of

_____   outstanding debt

_____   in addition to

_____   was willing to sacrifice

_____   went on to say

_____   in the near future

_____   any one of the two

_____   at the present time

_____	told his listeners that
_____	all of a sudden
_____	once in a great while
_____	a large number of
_____	during the time that
_____	at regular intervals of time
_____	tendered his resignation
_____	taken to jail and locked up
_____	ended his talk to the assembled audience with the following statement
_____	as long as (time, not space)
_____	not any one of the two
_____	was able to make his escape
_____	brought to a sudden halt
_____	completely destroyed by fire
_____	uniform in both size and shape
_____	in the same manner as
_____	made an investigation of
_____	is of the opinion that
_____	a great number of times

Possible answers (you may have others as well):

total	the sum amount due
immediately	as soon as possible
then, meanwhile	at that time

never	under no circumstances
once	on one occasion
when, whenever	whenever possible
few	a small number of
debt	outstanding debt
plus, also, additionally	in addition to
sacrificed	was willing to sacrifice
said, stated, continued	went on to say
soon	in the near future
either	any one of the two
now, presently	at the present time
said, stated, explained	told his listeners that
suddenly	all of a sudden
seldom, infrequently	once in a great while
many, multitude	a large number of
then, while	during the time that
regularly, frequently, intermittently	at regular intervals of time
resigned, quit	tendered his resignation
jailed, incarcerated,	taken to jail and locked up

concluded,
    summarized,
    finished, ended
	ended his talk to the assembled
	    audience with the
	    following statement

since	as long as (time, not space)
neither	not any one of the two
escaped	was able to make his escape
halted, stopped	brought to a sudden halt
razed	completely destroyed by fire
uniform, same,	uniform in both size and shape
like	in the same manner as
investigated	made an investigation of
thinks, feels, believes	is of the opinion that
many, several	a great number of times

REMOVING UNNECESSARY WORDS

See if you can eliminate wasted words in the following sentences:

1. When I think about it, it occurs to me that you may be right.

2. Your letter came at a time when we were busy.

3. Under no circumstances should customer preferences and opinions be ignored.

4. Our products depreciate in value slowly.

5. Needless to say, we are in dire financial straits — unable to even pay our bills when they are due.

6. During the year of 1990.

7. Regarding your recent letter per the question at hand.

8. It will cost the sum of $99.

9. Contrary to popular belief, the bankruptcy did not leave him completely broke and desolate.

10. We will ship your order at a later date.

11. One might wonder about the whereabouts of the unclaimed merchandise even now.

12. In about two weeks' time.

13. During the course of the campaign.

14. The car sells at a price of $12,000.

15. We are now engaged in building a new plant.

16. In the city of Cleveland.

17. Perhaps it may be that the price is too high.

18. This is our uniform and invariable rule.

19. With the means of your donation.

20. We see the defect in both of them.

ANSWERS:

1. You may be right.

2. Your letter came when we were busy.

3. Customer preferences should never be ignored.

4. Our products depreciate slowly.

5. We are insolvent.

6. During 1990.

7. Regarding your letter of _____.

8. It will cost $99.

9. The bankruptcy did not leave him desolate.

10. We will ship your order by (give the specific date).

11. Where is the unclaimed merchandise?

12. In about two weeks.

13. During the campaign.

14. The car sells for $12,000.

15. We are engaged in building a plant.

16. In Cleveland.

17. Perhaps the price is too high.

18. This is our rule.

19. With your donation.

20. We see the defect in both.

BREAKING UP LONG SENTENCES

Break up the following sentences so that they are more readable:

○ Charts are analyzed and coded in a timely fashion and sent on to doctors' files for completion within a few days of discharge which helps decrease delinquent charts.

○ Because of the complexities of the situation I have decided to pay the full assessment on the property and consequently I have directed the Board of Governors to begin proceedings to provide the Seal Company with adequate funds to cover this initial expense.

○ If this method of operation is to continue it does raise the issue of why we are marketing a similar product abroad; however, we could discuss it further in Washington, D.C. at our annual meeting.

Possible answers:

○ Charts are analyzed and coded in a timely fashion. They're sent to doctors' files for completion within a few days of discharge. This helps decrease delinquent charts.

○ Because of the complexities of the situation, I have decided to pay the full assessment on the property. Consequently, I have directed the Board of Governors to begin proceedings. This will provide the Seal Company with adequate funds to cover this initial expense.

○ If this method of operation is to continue, it does raise the issue of why we are marketing a similar product abroad. However, we could discuss it further in Washington, D.C. at our annual meeting.

CREATING LISTS

Look at these three sentences containing items in a series. See if you can turn them into lists.

> I would appreciate your cooperation when ordering and using audio-visual equipment: (1) place all orders directly with the Audio-Visual Department, *not* through the Center Directors; (2) you *must* notify us *at least* seven working days before use; (3) pick up *and return* all audio-visual equipment and supplies at the Center Director's desk so that others may use materials as needed.

> This system will help enhance our service by freeing up ticket counter and gate lines, allowing more personal attention for those passengers needing extra assistance, maximizing our service while keeping costs low, and offering 24-hour check-in service.

Membership on a monitoring team would require the person to commit three to four days' time, and to serve on the monitoring team for a school site designated for monitoring, 1990-1991.

How do your answers compare?

I would appreciate your cooperation when ordering and using audio-visual equipment:

- o Place all orders directly with the Audio-Visual Department, *not* through the Center Directors
- o Notify us *at least* seven working days before use
- o Pick up and *return* all audio-visual equipment and supplies at the Center Director's desk so that others may use materials as needed

This system will help enhance our service by:

- o Freeing up ticket counter and gate lines
- o Allowing more personal attention for those passengers needing extra assistance
- o Maximizing our service while keeping costs low, and offering 24-hour check-in service

Membership on a monitoring team would require the person to:

- o Commit three to four days' time
- o Serve on the monitoring team for a school site designated for monitoring, 1990-1991

APPENDICES

APPENDIX A: A COMPENDIUM OF
ENGLISH USAGE

APPENDIX B: EDITING AND
PROOFREADING MARKS

APPENDIX C: ADDITIONAL RESOURCES
FOR BUSINESS WRITERS

APPENDIX A

A Compendium of English Usage

WORD USAGE

The following is a selected list of commonly misused words

a, an	Use *a* before all words beginning with a consonant sound (including h); otherwise use *an*.
ability, capacity	"Ability" means the state of being able or the power to do something. "Capacity" is the power of receiving or containing.
about, approximately	"About" indicates a guess or rough estimate (about half full). "Approximately" implies accuracy (approximately 34.76 gallons).
above	Do not use above as a noun ("the above proves"). Avoid it as an adjective ("the above statement"). Avoid it as an adverb ("as stated above"). Do not use the awkward above-mentioned, afore-mentioned, or other such phrases. Preferably, restate the subject or use a synonym.
accept, except	"Accept" means to receive willingly, to agree with. "Except" means excluding.
accidentally	Not spelled accidently.
adapt, adopt	*Adapt* means to make suitable or to adjust to. To *adopt* is to choose or to select for one's own.
advise, inform	"Advise" means to offer counsel and suggestions (I advise you to sell that stock). "Inform" means to communicate information (I inform you that your shipment has not arrived yet).
affect, effect	"Affect" is a verb meaning to change or influence. "Effect" is a noun meaning result or outcome. "Effect" is also a verb meaning to bring about.
aggravate	"Aggravate" means to make worse. Don't use it as a synonym for "irritate," "annoy," or "provoke."

all of	The *of* is usually superfluous, except with pronouns. All the chips were defective. All of them were present.
all ready, already	*All ready* means everyone is ready; *already* means by this time.
all right	Always this form; never alright or allright.
all together, altogether	The phrase "all together" means that everyone is in the same location. "Altogether" means entirely.
allude, refer	To "allude" is to refer indirectly. To "refer" is to name.
alternate, alternative	The former denotes a substitution designated to take the place of another; the latter means an optional second choice if the first choice is unsatisfactory.
among	See between.
amount, number	*Amount* is used for things in bulk or mass, *number* for things which are countable (see fewer, less): a large amount of water a large number of desks
and/or	This is an awkward construction. Avoid it. NOT: Sally and/or John BUT: Sally, John, or both
anxious, eager	Use "anxious" when anxiety or worry is involved, not as a synonym for eager. "Eager" means highly desirous of something.
apt, liable, likely	*Likely* is the only one of these terms meaning probable. *Apt* implies having a tendency (usually unfortunate) and *liable* suggests the risk of unpleasant consequences. Liable also means responsible for in the sense of damages.
around	Do not use for "about" in the sense of approximately.
as	Avoid using *as* for since or because.
as, like	See like.
as per	Meaningless. Use according to or a synonym.
assure, ensure, insure, secure	According to Webster, all four of these words mean to make an outcome sure. *Ensure* implies a making certain and inevitable; *insure* stresses the taking of necessary measures beforehand to

	make a result certain or provide for any probable contingency; *assure* implies a making sure in mind by removing all doubt and suspense; and *secure* implies action taken to guard against attack or loss.
as to	Do not use for of or about:

> NOT: We are certain as to his identity.

| bad, badly | Be sure that you mean the adverb when you use it, especially after verbs like seem, appear, taste, smell and feel: |

> He feels bad. [He is physically ill.]

> He feels badly. [His ability to sense by touching is poor.]

balance, remainder, rest	Balance is used in the sense of equilibrium. Do not use it for rest or remainder in formal writing.
because of, due to	"Because of" means by reason of or on account of. (The radar failed because of a short circuit.) "Due to" means attributable to. (Due to his efforts, the radar was repaired in an hour.)
beside, besides	"Beside" means by the side of. "Besides" means in addition to.
between, among	Use "between" when writing of two things. Use "among" when writing of three or more.
bi-	This means every two. Thus bimonthly means occurring every two months. For twice a month, use semi-monthly.
big, large, great	"Big" is used to refer to bulk, mass, weight, or volume. "Large" is used with nouns indicating dimensions, extent, quantity, or capacity. "Great" is now used almost entirely to connote importance or eminence.
boundary	The correct form of spelling; not boundry.
can, may	"Can" implies ability; "may" implies permission.
cannot, can not	The correct form is now almost universally considered to be the single word *cannot*.
center, middle	These terms are not interchangeable. From its geometric definition, "center" retains, even in nontechnical contexts, the idea of a point around which everything else revolves or rotates. "Middle" is less precise, suggesting space rather than a point.

cite, quote; sight, site	The report writer uses cite or citation to mean a reference to another's work for illustration, explanation, or proof. Such a reference would be actually quoted only if the writer employed the original wording exactly. The homonyms cite, sight, and site are confused more in spelling than in meaning.
claim	Do not use claim for assert or maintain but only in the sense of to demand as being due.
common	See mutual.

communication,
   communica-
   tions
	Communication is the transmission of information from one mind to another. This transmission may be orally, by signs, by writing, etc. *Communications* has to do with systems or hardware devised for this transmission of information.

compare with, compare to	To *compare to* is to liken one thing to another; to *compare with* is to examine two things to determine similarities and differences.

> He compared the brain to a computer.

> He compared the advantages of the first plan with those of the second plan to help the committee in choosing between them.

complement, compliment	The first term means to *complete* or fill out; the second, to *praise*.
comprise	*Comprise* means *to include* or to embrace in the sense that the whole, which must be the subject, comprises the parts, which must be the objects. Thus, comprised of is incorrect.
continual, continuous	"Continual" means recurring frequently; "continuous" means occurring without interruption. Memory aid: "Continuous ends in OUS, which stands for 'one uninterrupted sequence.'"
contrast	We contrast one thing with another.

> He contrasted silver with gold.

> BUT: The contrast between silver and gold is great. Management presented a contrast to what employees had expected.

credible, credulous	See incredible.
data, datum	When "data" is used synonymously with "facts," it is plural. When it is used synonymously with "information," it is singular. The singular form

	"datum" has fallen out of popular use in technical writing.
different from	Never different than unless the object is a clause.

> This car is entirely different from the older model.
>
> BUT: The story was different than he remembered it.

differs	

> Silver differs from gold.
>
> BUT: I differ with that opinion.

discover	We discover that which is already in existence but unknown. We develop or produce synthetics, etc.
discrete, discreet	The former means *separate*; the latter means *prudent*.
disinterested, uninterested	"Disinterested" means impartial. "Uninterested" means indifferent, having no pleasure or delight in something.
due to, owing to	*Due to*, one of the most commonly misused terms, is an adjective and must refer definitely to a noun. Due to is used correctly when attributed to can be substituted. A safe general rule for the use of due to is to use some form of the verb to be before it or place it next to the noun it modifies. *Owing to*, which must modify a verb, is correctly used when because of can be substituted.
economic, economical	*Economic* refers to the science of economics (production, distribution, consumption); *economical* means frugal, not wasteful.
effective, efficient	A machine that's "effective" performs its intended function well. If it does this with a minimum of waste, expense, and unnecessary effort, then it's "efficient" as well.
e.g., i.e.	"e.g." means for example; "i.e." means in other words or that is. Avoid the use of either of these in business writing. Instead use the words "for example" or "that is."
electric, electrical	Use *electric* to describe anything in which electricity is actually present (for example, electric motor, heater, control); use *electrical* in the abstract sense of pertaining to electricity (for

example, an electrical engineer, the electrical industry) or in the figurative sense.

enable
The term enable means to give ability, to make able. Obviously, this word should be used only when ability is given.

end result
The term end result is redundant since the word result conveys the thought of the end. Perhaps a more precise term may be employed, such as *conclusion*.

ensure
See assure.

equally as
The word *as* used with the word *equally* creates redundancy.

> The new equipment is equally good.
>
> NOT: It is equally as good.

equipment, equipments
"Equipment" is both singular and plural. There is no such word as "equipments."

essential
Essential means something that is necessary for the existence of something else. For example, EAM equipment is an essential part of a computer. Essential should not be used synonymously with important, highly desirable, and similar expressions. The term essential is also an absolute adjective, and as such, an object cannot be more essential than another.

everyone, every one
"Everyone" means all people. "Every one" means each one.

factor
Not accurate for consideration or part, but "one of the elements that contribute to produce a result":

> NOT: Financing is an important factor in business.
>
> BUT: Good financing was an important factor in establishing this business.

farther, further
Farther applies to distances (and contains the word "far"); *further* denotes degree or extent.

> The plant is six miles farther east.
>
> The debt was further increased by another loan.

fewer, less
Fewer refers to countable objects; *less* refers to bulk or mass (see amount):

> less time to manage
>
> fewer accounts to audit

the field of	The phrase *the field of* is almost always unnecessary
	NOT: in the field of plastics
	BUT: in plastics
firm	Strictly speaking, this means a partnership, not a corporation. Use *company* or *corporation*.
flammable, inflammable	Prefer the short form.
foreseeable future	A foolish phrase "since none of the future, not even the next second, is foreseeable."
foreword	Spell it this way if you mean preface or introduction.
from . . . to	Redundant construction.
	NOT: The report holds from 50,000 to 60,000 technical terms.
	BUT: The report holds 50,000 to 60,000 technical terms.
good, bad	Overused words in writing—be more specific and descriptive.
healthful, healthy	*Healthful* means good for one's health; *healthy* means having good health.
	healthy child healthful exercise
	healthy body healthful climate
hindrance	Never hinderance.
hopefully	The phrase "hopefully the situation will improve" is ridiculous because the situation cannot be full of hope. "Hopefully we shall fly to Pittsburgh tomorrow" does not mean we can hope to be in Pittsburgh tomorrow. It means we shall fly there full of hope. Beware of "hopefully."
identical	One thing is *identical with* another, not to another.
impact	"Impact" does not mean to affect or influence. "To impact" means to drive or press closely into something. Avoid "impact" as a synonym for "effect."

imply, infer	*Imply* means to hint, to intimate, or to suggest; but exactly used, *infer* means to draw a conclusion from evidence. The writer or speaker implies; the reader or listener infers.

> He implied in his remarks that the company was not liable.
>
> I inferred from his speech that no one was to blame.

in, inside of, within	*In* denotes place, position, or location. It also means the end or limit of a given time, distance, quantity or degree.

> He will return in (at the end of) a month.

Within denotes some time short of the end. It also denotes distance, quantities or degrees short of a given distance, quantity, or degree. Do not use *inside of* for within.

> He was within two years of being promoted.

in, into	Generally *in* locates and *into* directs:

> The trouble is in accounts payable.
>
> The auditor had to go into the past books.

inasmuch as	This form is correct. It may be expressed more easily by *because, since,* or *for*.
incredible, incredulous	"Incredible" means not believable. "Incredulous" means not able to believe. Statements or assertions are "incredible"; people are "incredulous."
independent of	NOT independent from.
indispensable	Never indispensible, as it frequently appears.
information, data	See data.
insofar as	Never in so far or as or insofaras.
insure	See assure.
inter-, intra-	Often confused. *Inter-* means between (for example, intercollegiate); *intra-* means inside (for example, intracompany).
irregardless	A corruption of regardless.
irrelevant	Not spelled irrelevant.
is when, is where	Do not use these expressions to introduce a noun clause in a definitive statement:

> NOT: Evaporation is when . . .
>
> BUT: Evaporation occurs when . . .

its, it's, (its')	Its and it's are very frequently and very improperly interchanged. Its' is an improper form, perhaps an attempt at the plural possessive of it (which is their). *Its*, of course, is the possessive pronoun and *it's* a contraction of it is or it has.
-ize	Though the suffix -*ize* in the sense to make into can be useful in saving words (for example, pluralize for to form the plural of), avoid awkward or unnecessary applications of it (for example, finalize, directorize, accountize).
kind of, sort of	Colloquial for *somewhat* or *rather*.
laboratory	Not spelled labratory.
last, latest	*Last* means final; *latest* means most recent.
later, latter	Carelessly interchanged. *Later*, of course, means after in a time sense; *latter* means the second of two.
lay, lie	Perpetual troublemakers. *Lay* is transitive (requires an object) and means to place; *lie* is intransitive (can have no object) and means to recline:

> He lays the report on the table before . . .
>
> He laid the report on the table before . . .
>
> He had laid the report on the table . . .
>
> The report lies on the table.
>
> The report lay on the table this morning.
>
> The report has lain on the table all day.

leave, let	*Leave* implies departure, *let* implies permission:

> Leave the door open. [Don't close it.]
>
> Let the door open. [Permit it to open.]
>
> Let him close the door. [Permit him to close it.]
>
> Leave him close the door. [Incorrect.]
>
> Leave him to his thoughts. [Correct.]

less	See fewer.
lightening, lightning	*Lightening* means making lighter; *lightning* is the companion of thunder.
like, as	"Like" is still not accepted as a conjunction except when it introduces a noun not followed by a verb. (He builds bridges "like" a veteran architect.)
along the lines of, in the line of	Wasteful and usually meaningless:

> NOT: what we have in the line of suits
>
> BUT: what we have in suits
>
> NOT: along the lines of the new proposal
>
> BUT: like the new proposal

located	This word is a colloquialism and is unnecessary in defining the location of specific places. "The bank is located on Main Street" conveys nothing not said in "The bank is on Main Street." Correctly used, located is the past tense of locate in the sense of discovering the lcoation by hunting for it.
loose, lose	The former means free, the opposite of tight; the latter means to suffer a loss.
lots of, a lot of	Colloquial for many, much, a great many, a large number, and so forth.
materiel, material	"Materiel" is the equipment, apparatus, and supplies used by an organization. "Material" refers to the substances of which something is composed.
maximum, optimum	Strong words. Use them with restraint. They are not interchangeable. *Maximum* (greatest) output is not necessarily *optimum* (best) output.
miniature	Not spelled minature.
more preferable	The word preferable is itself a comparative; the addition of the word more causes redundancy.
most, almost	Do not use the adjective most for the adverb almost:

> NOT: most all the employees
>
> BUT: almost all the employees

mutual, common	Preferably *mutual* refers to two objects or persons, *common* to more than two.
needless to say	This expression is redundant because the speaker or writer who uses this phrase usually proceeds to state that which does not need saying.
none	Purists to the contrary, none is now generally treated as a plural. Use no one for emphasis.

> None of these programs work on the new computer.
>
> No one of them is error-free.

noted, notorious	People famous in a desirable way are "noted"; people with unsavory reputations are "notorious."
number	See amount.
a number, the number	A *number* generally refers to several persons or things and thus requires a plural verb; *the number* generally refers to a total and takes a singular verb:

> There are a number of problems.
>
> The number of solutions has increased.

-one	Write *-one* solid with any, every, and some, unless the one is stressed:

> Everyone must attend.
>
> Every one of us will attend.

only	Do not use for but:

> NOT: We would have met our quota only the holidays were upon us.

only, just	Misunderstanding can result from improper placement of these words in the word order. Better emphasis is obtained and possible confusion avoided by placing them next to the word they describe or limit:

> They only stored the explosive. [No manufacturing.]
>
> They stored only the explosive. [Nothing else.]
>
> The plant just produced 200 tons. [Recently produced.]
>
> The plant produced just 200 tons. [Only 200 tons.]

optimum	See maximum.
oral, verbal	These are not synonymous terms. *Oral* means by mouth or spoken. *Verbal* means with words— as opposed to by signs, illustrations, etc. Oral instructions almost certainly are verbal. Verbal instructions might well be in writing.
oriented, orientated	The former is preferred.
over, under	Do not use these words for more than and less than.
over, more than	"Over" implies position. Do not write "over" when you mean more than. (There are "more than" 100 installations worldwide. I would choose this system "over" any of the others).

overall	Overall is the correct form; the term over-all is not in use.
party, person, individual	Except in legal language, do not use party to refer to a single person. Use individual in the abstract sense ("the rights of the individual").
percent (%), percentage	Always one word; never per cent. Use the symbol for percent with tabular material, and the word percent throughout the text. Percentage should never be used with a number. 99 percent 99% (tabular) a small percentage
perfect	This is an incomparable word. Since it means without flaw, perfect can have no comparative or superlative.
performance	Not spelled preformance.
period of time, lapse of time	A redundancy, since the words period and lapse convey the idea of time.
perseverance	Not spelled perserverance.
personal, personnel	Often confused, probably through carelessness in spelling. A personal secretary attends to private, social, or nonbusiness affairs; a personnel manager selects new employees for a company. Singular in its original meaning of the human element of the process of manufacturing (as opposed to material), personnel now also has a plural meaning as a synonym for employees. All personnel were advised of the new benefits.
practicable, practical	"Practicable" means that which appears to be capable of being put into practice. "Practical" means that something is known to be doable based on past performance.
prescribe, proscribe	The former term means to lay down a directive; the latter means to forbid, denounce, or outlaw, generally by formal action.
prescription	Not spelled perscription.
presently, at present	"Presently" means soon; "at present" means now.
preventive maintenance	Not preventative.

principal, principle	"Principal" used as a noun means head of a school, a main participant, a sum of money. As an adjective, it means first or highest in rank, worth, or importance. A "principle" is a fundamental law, a basic truth.
proposition	Colloquial for proposal, offer, or plan.
prove	The past participle is *proved*, not proven.

> It was proved to my satisfaction.

qualified expert	Redundant, since an unqualified expert is no expert at all.
raise, rise (verbs)	*Raise* is transitive (requires an object) and means to lift. *Rise* is intransitive (can have no object) and means to get up or to go up:

> Raise the price. Inflation raised the price.
>
> The price is rising. The price rose.

real	In formal writing, avoid using real in the sense of very or really.
reason is because	Awkward and redundant. Use "The reason for . . . is that . . ."
reason why	Also redundant. Drop one or the other:

> This is the reason it failed.
>
> Here is why it failed.

record	All-time, new high, or even new is redundant with record in reference to an unprecedented level or degree.
regular	The word regular is redundant with any word that indicates periodic recurrence:

> A regular weekly meeting, a regular monthly review.
>
> NOT: A regular, periodic meeting.

respectfully, respectively	Embarrassing to the writer who confuses them. Both are overworked. *Respectfully* (meaning with respect) should be used as a complimentary close in a letter only when respect is justly due. *Respectively* (meaning each in the order given) requires the reader to backtrack in his reading.
said	As an adjective, suitable only in legal documents.
seasonable, seasonal	*Seasonable* means suitable to the season; *seasonal* means pertaining to or dependent upon the seasons:

> High sales are not seasonable in May.

> Most seasonal work is performed by part-time workers.

sewage, sewerage	*Sewage* is waste matter; *sewerage* is the disposal system.
set, sit	*Set* is transitive (requires an object) and means to put or place down. *Sit*, meaning to be seated, is intransitive (can have no object):

> Set the typewriter over there.

> He can sit as he works on the computer.

shall, will	These two words have become virtually interchangeable except in the most formal writing.
should, will	"Should" implies ought to, a belief. "Will" is a prediction.
situated	Like located, this word is generally superfluous in describing the location of specific places.
sort of	Colloquial for *somewhat* or *rather*.
specie, species	*Specie* means coin. *Species* (same form for singular and plural) means variety or category.
split infinitive	There is no longer any objection to splitting an infinitive if the resulting construction is clearer or less awkward:

> To better acquaint the stockholders . . . (Clear)

> Better to acquaint the stockholders . . . (Awkward)

> Marketing had failed seriously to halt the market erosion of the product. (Ambiguous. Clarify by inserting seriously after to—splitting the infinitive.)

> BUT: Entries are sufficiently informative to frequently obviate the necessity of going to the files (Reword: Frequently entries are sufficiently informative to obviate, or Entries are often sufficiently informative to obviate . . .)

stationary, stationery	The former term, an adjective, means standing still. The latter, a noun, means writing paper.
strata	Strata is the preferred plural of stratum, a layer of air, rock, or tissue.
temperament	Not spelled temperment.
temperature	High or low temperatures, not hold or cold temperatures. This term is misspelled when appearing as temperture.

that, which	Ideally, "that" is used with a restrictive clause — a clause absolutely necessary to the sentence. (This is the vessel "that" holds the acid).
	"Which" is used with a nonrestrictive clause — a clause that adds descriptive matter and is not necessary to the sentence "which" is typically preceded by a comma. (The steel vessel, "which" is used to hold acid, was lined with ceramic bricks.)
their, there, they're	Confused through carelessness, but confused nevertheless:

> They are in their places. [Plural possessive.]
>
> They belong in there. [Adverb of place.]
>
> They're not in the right place. [Contraction of they are.]

these kind	This and that are the only adjectives in the language with plural forms. They must agree in number with the nouns they modify:

> this kind, sort   these kinds, sorts
>
> that kind, sort   those kinds, sorts

to, too, two	Be careful in spelling these words.
toward, towards	*Toward* is the preferred form.
transpire	This is no synonym for happen. Transpire means to leak out or become known.

> It transpired during the final trial that the cashier had been embezzling company funds over the years.

try (noun)	Acceptable for effort or attempt but such usage is not preferable in formal writing.
type, type of	Avoid type as an adjective:

> NOT: This type report . . .
>
> BUT: This type of report . . .

unique	Unique means having no like or equal; it should not be compared. The same logic applies to optimum, maximum, square, circular, and so forth.

> NOT: The process was very unique.
>
> BUT: The process was very nearly unique.
>
> SIMILARLY: The figure was more nearly square.

usable	Rather than useable.

utilize	This is *not* a synonym for use. Utilize has a connotation of improvization, of employing something when something more desirable is not available.
very	Be sure it is useful; it is often unnecessary: Very is not of very much use in business writing. Sales were very much overestimated.
whether . . . or not	The *or not* is generally superfluous. Whether this is true, we do not know. BUT: We will finish this project, whether we get help or not.
which	See that, which.
while	While should be used to express *time relationships*. Its use for *though* is weak and for *and* or *but* is inaccurate: RIGHT: Don't move the computer while it is running. WEAK: Delegating is best, while assigning adequate. POOR: Their work is completed, while ours is just begun.
whose	The use of whose for things as well as persons is now generally acceptable.

CAPITALIZATION

The two most important rules to follow in capitalization are:

○ Be consistent

○ When in doubt, don't

The tendency to over-capitalize is most prevalent. Three guides cover most instances: (1) that each sentence begin with a capital letter, (2) that each phrase in an enumeration begin with a capital letter, and (3) that every proper name or word derived from a proper name begins with a capital letter.

As further explanation for item 2, always capitalize when enumeration is presented in columns, regardless of whether bullets or digital enumerations are used.

New employees

- ○ Attend orientation
- ○ Enroll for benefits
- ○ Meet with personnel

Capitalization should distinguish the specific from the general, the proper from the common:

Senator Tower	a former senator
France	a country, a European country
the English language	any modern language
Xerox Corporation	a closed corporation
Fig. 12, Figure 12	the figure

The following rules answer the most frequent questions about capitalizing.

FIRST WORD OF A SENTENCE

Capitalize the first word of a sentence—including a sentence in quotation:

The manager asked for a complete report.
The president reported, "Four men were promoted to executives."

FIRST WORD OF A DIRECT QUESTION   Capitalize the first word of a direct question whether or not it is part of another sentence:

What should the business writer ask himself?

The effective business writer asks himself, Who will read this report? What does he already know? What must he be told?

To the question, What next? there are three answers.

Three questions must be answered: Who? Where? When?

FRAGMENTARY QUOTATION   Do not capitalize a fragmentary quotation or the resumption of a separated quotation:

The president reported (that) four men will be promoted.
"Four men," the president reported, "will be promoted."

FIRST WORD FOLLOWING A COLON   Do not capitalize the first word following a colon when it begins a statement which amplifies, illustrates, or supports the preceding statement.

FIRST WORD OF AN EXPRESSION   Do not capitalize the first word of an expression in parentheses unless the enclosed expression constitutes the entire sentence.

PRINCIPAL WORDS

Capitalize the principal words (including the first and last) in titles of publications, articles, speeches, and so forth:

The Theory of the Financial Investing
"Understanding the Stock Market"

TITLES

Capitalize titles used in place of specific names already identified:

Vice President Smith   BUT: one of the vice presidents

the Director (of a   a research director
particular laboratory)

TITLE OF HONOR

Capitalize a title of honor or respect either immediately preceding or following a proper name:

Judge Wapner
Professor E. McCloud
Dean Johnson
Dr. John A. Hubert, Vice President, North American Can

NAMES OF COMPANIES

Capitalize names of companies, organizations, or institutions—and their abbreviations, if any:

UniSys
Columbia Broadcasting System (CBS)
United Parcel Service (UPS)
American Society for Training and Development (ASTD)
Occupational Safety and Hazard Administration (OSHA)

POINTS OF THE COMPASS

Capitalize points of the compass only when they designate specific areas:

the West   west of the Mississippi
the Middle West   six blocks south
the Far East   facing south
North vs. South   southeastern Utah

DAYS OF THE WEEK

Capitalize days of the week, holidays, and months.

Monday   Labor Day   Easter   September

Do not capitalize seasons:

fall

ACADEMIC DEGREES

Capitalize abbreviations of academic degrees and similar distinctions:

M.D.   C.E.   Ph.D M.P.

FIGURE AND TABLE

Capitalize Fig., Table, No., and Vol. when they refer to a specific numbered item:

Fig. 5   Table I   No. 5   Vol. 24

REGISTERED TRADEMARKS

Capitalize registered trademarks:

Kodacolor   Sunoco   Mustang   Norelco

USE OF TRADEMARKS When used to identify the source of a product, the trademark must be prominently displayed on the product. All other uses of the trademark, for example, in advertising, in publications, on containers or packages, must include an appropriate superscript ("TM" or "R") immediately following the trademark:

○ Until a registration is obtained in the U.S. Patent Office
  the superscript ™ must be used.

○ After registration is obtained the superscript ® must
  be used.

Special procedures for using trademarks in publications and advertising:

○ The trademark should be distinguished from the rest of
  the text, for example, by capitalization.

○ The trademark should always be used as a modifier or
  adjective.

○ The first or most prominent use of the trademark should
  include the appropriate superscript ("TM" or "R").

HYPHENATION

The business writer neglects no tool more than the hyphen. His primary need for it is to show that two or more units (usually words) function as one. Its absence can slow, even stop a reader:

no smoking signs	dual system of payment rule
break even point	the make-work rule attempts to . . .
low cost or free installation	operating experience statistics

Its presence can change the meaning:

a large scale map	[a large map drawn to scale]
a large-scale map	[a map drawn to large scale]
five gallon containers	[five containers of one-gallon capacity]
five-gallon containers	[containers holding five gallons]
foreign car buyers	[foreign buyers of cars]
foreign-car buyers	[buyers of foreign cars]

COMPOUND ADJECTIVES

Hyphenate compound adjectives:

well-placed emphasis	fast-starting meeting
door-to-door canvass	alternating-current motor
10-ton truck	never-to-be-forgotten experiment
well-known engineer	a 2- to 100-kc peak signal

In business writing, the compound adjective formed from a quantity and a unit is extremely common:

eight-hour day	¼-hp motor
90-acre lot	one-man operation
12-quart capacity	1500-degree range

NOTE: Instead of repeating the unit in a series of such compounds, it is included only in the last compound and a comma substituted elsewhere:

first-, second-, and third-shift workers
4-, 8-, and 12-ft lengths

ADVERBS ENDING IN -LY Adverbs ending in -ly do not form compound adjectives:

well-known engineer	BUT: widely known engineer
fast-moving inventory	BUT: rapidly moving inventory

PREDICATIVE POSITION Adjectives which should be hyphenated before a noun should not be hyphenated in the predicative position (where actually they become adverb and adjective, adjective and noun, and so on):

Dr. Sauer is a well-known consultant.
The device requires an alternating-current motor.

BUT:

Dr. Sauer is well known as a consultant.
The motor for this device uses alternating current.

SPELLED-OUT COMPOUND NUMBERS

Hyphenate spelled-out compound numbers from twenty-one to ninety-nine whether used alone or in combination:

thirty-three   one hundred thirty-three   thirty-three hundredths

MIXED NUMBERS

Hyphenate mixed numbers and spelled-out fractions:

1-³⁄₁₆ (NOT 1 ³⁄₁₆)   five-eighths   one-fourth

PREFIXES SELF- AND QUASI-

Always use a hyphen after the prefixes self- and quasi-; use a hyphen after ex- in the sense of former:

self-actuating   quasi-corporation   ex-manager

PROPER NAMES

Compounds are hyphenated when the second element is capitalized or considered as representing something official or institutional:

pro-United Nations   ex-governer

PREPOSITIONAL PHRASES

Compounds are hyphenated when containing a prepositional phrase:

behind-the-scenes agreement
over-the-counter stocks
state-of-the-art graphics

DIVIDING A WORD

Use a hyphen when it is necessary to divide a word at the right-hand margin. Divide, of course, only between syllables.

NUMBERS

GENERAL PRINCIPLE

In business writing, prefer figures to spelled-out numbers. Sometimes, however, appearance, consistency, or clarity is better served by the longer form. The following specific rules often apply to ordinal as well as cardinal numbers.

SPELL OUT

WHOLE NUMBERS UNDER 10   Whole numbers under 10 when used in text [Exception: 2.2]:

> Marketing conducts six surveys a month.
> The sixth survey is of existing customers.

NUMBERS BEGINNING SENTENCES   Numbers beginning sentences, captions, or headings, and numbers related to and closely following them:

> Forty percent is refunded.
>
> Twenty managers will be needed.
>
> Twenty chemists and twenty-five engineers . . .
>
> Fifty years of expansion . . .
>
> BUT: 1960 Production Costs. [Large numbers in captions and headings are represented by figures.]

Suggestion: By rewording, move the number into the sentence:

> The job will require 20 chemists and 25 engineers.

ROUND-NUMBER APPROXIMATIONS   Numbers representing round-number approximations or indefinite expressions:

> about thirty years old
> two or three thousand units per day
> less than a thousand dollars a week
> the early thirties

NOTE: The words about, approximately, nearly, and so forth, are not usually considered introducers of indefinite expressions in this sense:

> nearly 14 years
> almost 30 hours
> approximately a thousand man-hours

TWO ADJACENT NUMBERS   The first (sometimes the shorter) of two adjacent numbers not separated by punctuation:

three 110-volt transformers

BUT March 21, 1940

The production supervisors were expected to work twenty 12-hour shifts.

The order called for 126 forty-foot lengths.

USE FIGURES FOR

NUMBERS OVER NINE   Numbers over nine [Exceptions: 1.2]:

10   278   2817   12,463

RELATED NUMBERS   Related numbers in a sentence or consecutive sentences when one or more are larger than nine:

The crude came from 16 fields, 5 of them foreign.
The researcher takes 4, 8, or 12 samples daily.
The vehicles are designed for 8-, 10-, or 12-man crews.

SERIAL NUMBERS   Serial numbers and numbered objects:

Model 07946	Paragraph 17
Figure 5	Generator No. 4
Ohio Route 45	Part 23676593
Chapter 2	Pages 9-13

DECIMALS

2.763   0.114   0.27 inch   13.32 inches   12.7 in.

NOTE: Prefer decimals to all but the commonest fractions except in business where fractions are customary (for example, the clothing and the construction industries). Decimals are simpler to read, type, or print.

○ Place a cipher before a decimal less than unity:

0.11   0.732   0.2143

○ Place ciphers after a decimal point or after the last figure to the right only when needed for exactness or consistency:

$24,000 NOT $24,000.00
BUT: at a unit cost of 0.002
    at a unit cost of 0.0030 [If 4th place is significant.]
    either $2.00 or $2.02 per thousand

FRACTIONS   Fractions and mixed numbers:

½-in. pipe   1-¼ to 1-¾ tons   ⅔-hr intervals

○ Major exception: Fractions standing alone (not followed immediately by a unit) should be spelled out:

one-tenth as large
three-eights of an inch
two-thirds turn
three thirty-seconds

○ Use figures for fractions in compound modifiers:

¼-hp motor   ⅒-sec intervals

○ In typing mixed numbers, separate the integer from the fraction by a hyphen to prevent misreading:

1-⁵⁄₁₆ NOT 1 ⁵⁄₁₆ [which could be read ¹⁵⁄₁₆]

PERCENTAGES   Percentages, proportion, ratio:

11.6 percent	79-½ percent	0.2 percent
1:3 [often: 1 to 3]	1:3:5	1:50,000

NOTE: Percent is always spelled out as one word, except in tabular material, when it is used as the percent sign (%).

NUMBERS IN COMPOUND MODIFIERS   Most numbers in compound modifiers

12-cycle motor   9-ft radius*   10-hour shift

NUMBERS IN TABLES   All numbers appearing in tables, diagrams, graphs. (Lower-case letters are used for footnote indexes in tabular matter to avoid confusion with exponents.)

UNITS OF MEASUREMENT   Units of measurement, quantity, and time:

8 by 12 inches	12 tons	57 cents	12 noon
9 × 12 in.	20/20 vision	6 centimeters	8:50 p.m.
$1450 NOT	$1450 dollars	OR	1450 dollars
August 12, 1910	August 1918	12 August 1910	August 12
BUT: Fourth of July			
60 years old	14 years 6 months 5 days		

NOTE: For large numbers in text use the words million, billion, and so forth.

185 million persons $340 billion

NUMBERS ON DIALS   To refer to numbers appearing on dials, scales, and so forth:

Meter readings of 3.0, 3.5, and 4.1 were . . .
When the needle drops below 0, recalibrate.

---

*In technical writing, standard abbreviations are often used in such compounds.

NOTE: Where misreading could result, spell out.

HOUSE NUMBERS   For house numbers (except one), and for street names requiring more than one word:

    439 West Prospect Avenue
    9 First Street NW
    502 East 101st Street
    70 Twenty-Second Avenue
    One Embarcadero Square

PUNCTUATION OF NUMBERS

FOUR-DIGIT NUMBER   Omit the comma from a four-digit number:

    1347   2932   1818   BUT   27,032

NOTE: For alignment, the comma is inserted in four-digit numbers appearing in columns containing larger numbers.

SERIAL NUMBERS   Commas are generally omitted from serial numbers regardless of length:

    Part No. 1642913D   Engine 27483

RATIOS   Use a colon to express ratios.

HYPHEN   Use a hyphen in mixed numbers, spelled-out fractions, and in compound numbers 21 through 99 if they must be spelled out.

○ In mixed numbers:

    27-$\frac{3}{4}$ 1-$\frac{5}{16}$

○ In spelled-out fractions (unless part of the fraction already contains a hyphen):

    three-fourths   seven-eights   BUT   three thirty-seconds

○ In compound numbers from 21 to 99 if they must be spelled out:

    ninety-nine   one hundred ninety-nine

MISCELLANEOUS NUMBER PROBLEMS

UNITS IN A SERIES   Do not repeat units in a series unless they are represented by symbols:

    loads of 6, 8, 10, and 14 tons   BUT   priced at $6, $8, $9, and $12

FRACTIONAL UNITS   Use the singular form of a unit following fractions or decimals less than unity. Most abbreviations have no plural form.

    0.15 mile $\frac{5}{16}$ in. $\frac{2}{3}$ lb   BUT   2.7 inches

SPELLED-OUT NUMBER   Except in legal documents, do not repeat a spelled-out number in figures or vice versa:

> $21,000. NOT $21,000 (twenty-one thousand dollars)
> seven men NOT seven (7) men

ROMAN NUMERALS   Avoid Roman numerals unless two numbering systems are required for differentiation.

PUNCTUATION

Punctuation clarifies the meaning of written or printed language. Well-planned word order requires a minimum of punctuation.

PERIOD

The period is used:
    After a declarative sentence that is not exclamatory or after an imperative sentence.

> Stars are suns.
> He was employed by Sampson & Co.
> Do not be late.

After an indirect question or after a question intended as a suggestion and not requiring an answer.

> Tell me how he did it.
> May we hear from you.
> May we ask prompt payment.

SEMICOLON

A semicolon indicates a pause that is stronger than a comma but weaker than a period.
    The semicolon is used:
    To connect two complete sentences that are so closely related in meaning that they should be in one sentence.

> The cafeteria closes at 4:00; the dining room remains open until 8:00.
> Central High wins often; Lincoln High usually loses.

Instead of a comma to separate items that are especially long, or items that have commas within them.

> She wore a red, pleated, designer skirt; a white, long-sleeved, designer blouse; and medium-heeled, navy, designer pumps.

To separate clauses containing commas.

Donald A. Peters, president of the First National Bank, was also a director of New York Central; Harvey D. Jones was a director of Oregon Steel Co. and New York Central; Thomas W. Harrison, chairman of the board of McBride & Co., was also on the board of Oregon Steel Co.

COLON

The colon is used:

Before a final clause that extends or amplifies preceding matter.

Computers are no longer a luxury in business: they are a necessity.

To introduce formally any matter that forms a complete sentence, question, or quotation.

The following question came up for discussion: what policy should be adopted?

He said:

There are three factors, as follows: First, military preparation; second, industrial mobilization; and third, manpower.

After a salutation.

Dear Sir:

To Whom It May Concern:

In expressing clock time.

2:40 p.m.

In bibliographic references, between place of publication and name of publisher.

Congressional Directory. Washington: U.S. Government Printing Office.

To separate book titles and subtitles.

Financial Aid for College Students: Graduate
Germany Revisited: Education in the Federal Republic

COMMA

The comma is used:

To separate two words or figures that might otherwise be misunderstood.

Instead of hundreds, thousands came.
Instead of 20, 50 came.
February 10, 1987.
In 1930, 400 men were dismissed.

Before a direct quotation of only a few words following an introductory phrase.

He said, "Now or never."

After each of a series of coordinate qualifying words.

short, swift memos

but

short tributary streams

To set off parenthetic words, phrases or clauses.

Mr. Jefferson, who was then Secretary of State, favored the location of the National Capital at Washington.

It must be remembered, however, that the Government had no guarantee.

It is obvious, therefore, that this office cannot function.

but

The man who fell (restrictive clause) broke his back.
The dam that gave way (restrictive clause) was poorly constructed.
He therefore gave up the search.

To set off words or phrases in apposition or in contrast.

Mr. Green, the lawyer, spoke for the defense.
Mr. Jones, attorney for the plaintiff, signed the petition.
Mr. Smith, not Mr. Black, was elected.

After each member within a series of three or more words, phrases, letters, or figures used with "and," "or," or "nor."

red, white, and blue
by the bolt, by the yard, or in remnants
a, b, and c
neither snow, rain, nor heat

Before the conjunction in a compound sentence.

Fish, mollusks, and crustaceans were plentiful in the lakes, and turtles frequented the shores.
The boy went home alone, and his sister remained with the crowd.

After a noun or phrase in direct address.

Senator, will the measure be defeated?
Mr. Chairman, I will reply to the gentleman later.

Between title of person and name of organization in the absence of the words "of" or "of the."

Chief, Division of Finance
chairman, Committee on Appropriations
president, San Diego State University

Inside closing quotation mark.

He said "four," not "five."
"Freedom is an inherent right," he insisted.
"I work here," she said.

To separate thousands, millions, etc., in numbers of four or more digits.

4,230   50,491   1,250,000

After the year in complete dates within sentence.

The reported dates of September 11, 1986, to June 12, 1987, were
erroneous.

This was reflected in the June 13, 1987, report.

but

Production for June 1987 was normal.

DASH

The dash is used:
  To mark a sudden break or abrupt change in thought.

He said—and no one contradicted him—"The battle is lost."
If the bill should pass—which it should—the service will be wrecked.

Instead of commas or parentheses, if the meaning may thus
be clarified.

These are shore deposits—gravel, sand, and clay—but marine sediments
underlie them.

To precede a credit line or a run-in credit or signature.

Still achieving, still pursuing,
Learn to labor and to wait.
                    —Longfellow.

Every man's work shall be made manifest.—Corinthians 3:13.
This statement is open to question.—Gerald H. Forsythe.

DASH AND HYPHEN

Don't confuse the dash and the hyphen:
  Use a DASH (twice as long as a hyphen) to indicate a sudden
pause in a sentence.

Use a set of dashes around a parenthetical expression. Don't overdo the use of the dash!

The hyphen is used:

To connect the elements of certain compound words.

To indicate continuation of a word divided at end of a line.

Between the letters of a spelled word.

> The Style Board changed the spelling a-l-i-n-e to a-l-i-g-n.

The hyphen, as an element, may be used to represent letters deleted or illegible words in copy.

> d--n   h-ll   Leroy Joseph B---

PARENTHESES

Parentheses are used:

To set off matter not intended to be part of the main statement or not a grammatical element of the sentence, yet important enough to be included.

> This case (124 U.S. 329) is not relevant.

To enclose a parenthetic clause where the interruption is too great to be indicated by commas.

> You can find it neither in French dictionaries (at any rate, not in Larousse) nor in English.

To enclose an explanatory word not part of a written or printed statement.

> the Erie (PA) News; but the News of Erie, PA
> Portland (OR) Chamber of Commerce; but Washington, DC, schools

To enclose letters or numbers designating items in a series, either at beginning of paragraphs or within a paragraph.

> The order of delivery will be: (a) food, (b) clothing, and (c) tents and other housing equipment.
> You will observe that the sword is: (1) old fashioned, (2) still sharp, and (3) unusually light for its size.

To enclose a figure inserted to confirm a written or printed statement given in words if double form is specifically requested.

> This contract shall be completed in sixty (60) days.

A reference in parentheses at the end of a sentence is placed before the period, unless it is a complete sentence in itself.

The specimen exhibits both phases (pl. 14, A, B).
The individual cavities show great variation. (See pl.4).

Note position of period relative to closing parenthesis:

The vending stand sells a variety of items (sandwiches, beverages, cakes, etc.).

The vending stand sells a variety of items (sandwiches, beverages, cakes, etc. (sometimes ice cream)).

QUOTATION MARKS

Quotation marks are used:

To enclose quoted material. Only the exact words are placed inside quotation marks. Be sure to use a complete set: a pair at the beginning, a pair at the end. Don't use quotation marks to enclose an indirect quotation.

He said, "I think Dan's lying."
He said he thought Dan was lying.

Outside commas and periods.

"I wanted to go for a walk," he said, "but it started to snow."

Inside colons and semicolons.

Jan said, "I'm going"; Pete said, "I'm not."

Outside question marks and exclamation points when they are part of the quoted material. Place quotation marks inside if the question marks or exclamation points are part of the whole sentence.

Should I believe, "All that glitters is not gold"?
He asked, "Is Ella home?"

Around names of short works—poems, songs, short stories, etc. (Underline or italicize names of longer works—plays, books, newspapers, magazines, etc.)

"Trees"   "Yesterday"   "The Lottery"

Around nicknames, slang and colloquial expression, foreign phrases and technical terms, but don't overdo it.

To enclose direct quotations. (Each part of an interrupted quotation begins and ends with quotation marks.)

The answer is "No."
He said, "John said, 'No.'"
"John," said Henry, "Why do you go?"

APOSTROPHES AND POSSESSIVES

The possessive case of a singular or plural noun not ending in "s" is formed by adding an apostrophe and "s." The possessive case of a singular or plural noun ending is "s" or with an "s" sound is formed by adding an apostrophe only.

Man's, men's
prince's, princes'
Essex's, Essexes'
hostess', hostesses'
Jones', Joneses'
Jesus'

Possessive pronouns do not take an apostrophe.

its   ours   theirs

Possessive indefinite or impersonal pronouns require an apostrophe.

each other's books
one's home
someone's pen
somebody else's proposal

The singular case is used in such general terms as the following:

arm's length
attorney's fees
author's alterations
confectioner's sugar
cow's milk

In addition to illustrating possession, an apostrophe is used to indicate contractions, the omission of figures or letters.

don't
I've
it's (it is) (it has)
class of '92
spirit of '76
three R's
4-H'ers
49'ers

ELLIPSES

Three asterisks or three periods, are used to denote an ellipsis within a sentence, at the beginning or end of a sentence, or in two or more consecutive sentences when material has been left out.

"During the past twenty-five years . . . we have been witnessing a
change in buying habits."

Can anyone explain why . . . ?

QUESTION MARK

The question mark is used:
   To indicate a direct query, even if not in the form of a question.

Did he do it?
He did what?
Who asked, "why?" (Note single question mark)
"Did you hurt yourself, my son?" she asked.

EXCLAMATION POINT

The exclamation point is used to mark surprise, incredulity, admira-
tion, appeal, or other strong emotion, which may be expressed even in
a declarative or interrogative sentence.

He acknowledged the error!
How beautiful!
What!
"Great!" he shouted. (Note omission of comma.)
Who shouted, "All aboard!" (Note omission of question mark.)

ABBREVIATIONS

Abbreviations should be avoided whenever possible in business writing, although the use of standard abbreviations is permissible.

Abbreviations serve as a form of shorthand as long as they remain
familiar to the reader. However, the space saved by using them does
not compensate for the loss of clarity resulting from the use of those
abbreviations which are unfamiliar to the reader.

In business and industry the writer is permitted considerable freedom in using abbreviations. Even so, he must use only those recognized as standard by the dictionary, by the government, or by his
industry or profession.

If there exists any doubt about the reader's recognition of an
abbreviation, then the word should be spelled out in full and the
abbreviation placed along side within parentheses the first time the
word occurs in the text. Thereafter, the abbreviation will suffice.

Reference: United States Goverment Printing Office, Style Manual, March 1984.
The Gregg Reference Manual, 6th ed., New York: McGraw-Hill, 1984.

Spell out references in text (not parenthetical or footnote citations) to chapters, pages, lines, notes, verses, figures, and plates.

The excerpt is located on page 43, line 22

Application of this financial theory is demonstrated on page 82, Figure 12-4

When "and" connects descriptive words, it should be spelled out.

The American Telephone and Telegraph Company
The American Steel and Wire Company

Following are additional specific rules for abbreviations:

1. In text, do not use an abbreviation unless a quantity expressed in numeral form precedes it.

2. Do not abbreviate short words like day, mile, rod, ton, acre, cent, chain, liter, week.

3. Most abbreviations have no plural form [Exceptions: pp. (pages), mos. (months), nos. (numbers), vols. (volumes), yrs. (years)]:

15 in.   30 lb   55 mph   44 sq cm

4. Omit the period after technical abbreviations unless the resulting form constitutes a word:

ft   hp   psi   Btu   *BUT*   in.   at.wt

5. Capitalize letters in abbreviations only when they represent proper nouns or adjectives [Exception: C for centigrade]:

| 60-hp motor | NOT | 60 HP or 60 H. P. |
| 1600 Btu | NOT | 1600 BTU or B. T. U. |

6. Generally omit both periods and spacing in abbreviating organization names:

ASA   ASME   ASTM   ICC   TVA   *BUT*   U.S.   U.N.

7. In street addresses spell out North, South, East, West, Street, Avenue, and so forth, but abbreviate sectional divisions of a city such as NW, SE:

439 West Prospect Avenue   33 Pennsylvania Avenue NW

8. Abbreviate compass directions:

N   E   S   W   SW   NNW   12°N   25°W

9. Do not abbreviate Brothers, Company, Corporation, Limited, Railroad, and so forth unless the company itself abbreviates it.

10. Do not abbreviate city names:

WRONG: Phila.   L.A.   K.C.   N.Y.

11. Spell out May, June, and July. Abbreviate other months, if at all, only when the day is given:

August 1910   August 12, 1910   12 August 1910 (military usage)

12. Avoid using conventional signs: % for percent, # for space or number, ' for feet or minutes, / for per in text. [Exceptions: Intra-industry communications sometimes violate these rules. For example, B/D for barrels per day is widely used in the petroleum industry but should not be used for readers outside the industry. The dollar sign is the major exception when accompanied by a numeral, and x is often acceptable for by in giving dimensions.]:

9 in.   10 ft   10 sec $63   4 × 6 × 12 in.

SPELLING

Following are seven basic rules for better spelling:

RULE I—I BEFORE E

A. Use i before e in words with ie or ei when the sound is long ee, except after c or when sounded as a as in neighbor and weight. (convenience, believe, achieve)

B. Generally use e before i when the sound is not long ee, unless the sound of i is distinctly pronounced first. (height, foreign)

C. Use i before e in the sound of "sh." (efficiency, sufficient)

D. Exceptions: either, neither, leisure, friend, plebeian, protein, seize, weird.

RULE II—SILENT E

A. Drop the silent e at the end of a word before a suffix beginning with a vowel. (advertise-advertising, compare-comparative, use-usable)

C. Retain the silent e at the end of a word before a suffix beginning with a consonant. (require-requirement, sincere-sincerely, hope-hopeful)

D. Retain the silent e preceded by c or g to keep a "soft" sound with suffix endings beginning with a or o. (The g already has a "soft" sound when preceded by d to form dg, such as knowledgable and judging.)

E. Exceptions: argument, awful, duly, mileage, ninth, truly, wisdom.

RULE III—DOUBLE CONSONANT

A. Double the final consonant before a suffix beginning with a vowel in words of one syllable and in words accented on the last syllable ending in a single consonant preceded by a single vowel (plan-planned, confer-conferred, occur-occurrence). Exception: words ending in x.

B. Do not double the final consonant before a suffix beginning with a consonant, when the final consonant is not preceded by a single vowel, or when the accent is not on the last syllable. (equip-equipment, initial-initialed, benefit-benefited)

C. Exceptions: busing, gases, handicapped, transferable, transferred.

RULE IV—Y TO I

A. Change the y to i before a suffix ending (except an ending beginning with i) in words ending in y preceded by a consonant. (company-companies, likely-likelihood, simplify-simplifying)

B. Retain the y when adding any suffix or the letter s in words ending in y preceded by a *vowel*. (attorney-attorneys, enjoy-enjoyment)

C. Exceptions: day-daily, gay-gaily, pay-paid.

RULE V—CEDE, CEED, SEDE

A. Only one word ends in -sede: supersede.

B. Three words end in -ceed: exceed, succeed, proceed.

C. All the rest end in -cede. (concede, intercede, precede, etc.).

RULE VI—IZE, ISE, YZE

A. Of these endings, -ize is the most common. Usually when the first part of the word is a word in itself, use -ize. (apology-apologize, emphasis-emphasize, standard-standardize)

B. When the first part of the word is not a word in itself, use -ise. (advertise, enterprise, supervise)

C. Four words end in -yze: analyze, paralyze, dialyze, catalyze.

RULE VII—ABLE OR IBLE

To determine whether an adjective should end in -able or -ible, call to mind the noun form.

A. Usually if the noun form ends in -ation, use -able. (application-applicable, consideration-considerable, imagination-imaginable)

B. If the noun form ends in -ion or -tion (but not -ation), use -ible. (collection-collectible, deduction-deductible, permission-permissible) Many words ending in -able and -ible are not governed by this rule. When in doubt, consult a good dictionary.

Source: W. E. Perkins and Melba Benson, "Great Disasters of the Twentieth Century," *Journal of Business Education* (December, 1979), pp. 98–103.

APPENDIX B

Editing and Proofreading Marks

Mark Used	Correction Indicated	Example of Mark Used Within Copy
˩ or ˥ or ˢ	Delete	When in⌐ the course
	Delete and close up	When in th℮ course
	Close up, no space	space borne capsule
#	Leave space	performed within
⌗	Close up to one space	When # in the
[	Move to left	[with the computer
]	Move to right	With the computer]
⌐	Move up	With the computer
⌐	Move down	With the computer
⊗	Replace imperfect type	Computer
¶	Make new paragraph	computer. ¶ The module
no ¶	Run into same paragraph	side effects. The language is then
sp	Spell out	75% of inventory
sp?	Check spelling	bookkeeper sp?
cap(s)	Capitalize	Apple computer
lc	Place in lower case	a Computer was
cap & lc	Capitalize first letter	USA TODAY
⌄	Insert comma	computer display and other
⌄	Insert apostrophe or single quote	managements intention
⌄/⌄	Insert quotation marks	entitled Physical Characteristics
⌃	Insert period	console Thus, the
⌃	Insert colon	the following shift right, shift left
⌃	Insert semicolon	control this would include
⌃	Insert parenthesis	criteria similar to the preceding
⌃	Insert question mark	ask "When will it stop"
⌃	Insert hyphen	heavy duty equipment
⎯⎯/	Underscore	the word Display
⌄	Set as subscript	A3
⌃	Set as superscript	10−8
tr	Transpose letters or words	or following the
stet	Restore word crossed out, ignore correction	anticipated slippages STET
insert	Insert omitted material*	When the became
↶	Move to position indicated	impedance too high became
‖ or =	Align	‖Computer peripherals ‖Display

*When lengthy material is to be added, use a circled letter (Ⓐ) and attach separate page.

APPENDIX C

Additional Resources for Business Writers

The most important resource any writer needs is a good dictionary. We recommend *Webster's New World Dictionary of the American Language*, although most current dictionaries will suffice. Consult your dictionary often for clarificatioin and confirmation. Other resources you may find of value include:

Bates, Jefferson D. *Writing With Precision*. Washington, D.C.: Acropolis Books, 1978.

Briggs, James I. *The Berkeley Guide to Employment for New College Graduates*. (Compiled and edited by Robert B. Nelson) Berkeley: Ten Speed Press, 1984.

Buzan, Tony. *Use Both Sides of Your Brain*. New York: E.P. Dutton, 1983. New techniques on reading, studying and thinking. Includes an excellent discussion of mind-mapping.

Colby, John and Rice, Joseph A. *Writing to Express*. Minneapolis: Burgess Publishing, 1977.

Directory of Editorial Resources: The Best Books, Directories, Periodicals, Professional Organizations, Training Opportunities, Grammar Hotlines for Writers and Editors. This excellent annual directory is available from Editorial Experts, Inc., 85 S. Bragg Street, Alexandria, VA, 22312, (703) 642-3040 for $11.50 (as of this writing), which includes postage and handling.

Flesch, Rudolf. *The Art of Readable Writing*. New York: Collier/Macmillian, 1949. The classic work on writing readability and how to improve it.

Glatthorn, Allan A. *Writing for Success*. Glenview, Ill.: Scott, Foresman and Co., 1985.

Hodges, John C., with Whitten, Mary E., in consultation with Connolly, Francis X. *Harbrace College Handbook*. New York: Harcourt, Brace & World, 1962. One of the most comprehensive and correct guides for the individual writer and college instructor.

Jacoby, James W. *How to Prepare Managerial Communications*. Washington, D.C.: The Bureau of National Affairs, 1983.

Mack, Karin and Skjei, Eric. *Overcoming Writing Blocks*. Los Angeles: J.P. Tarcher, 1979.

Manhard, Stephen J. *The Goofproofer: How to Avoid the 41 Most Embarrassing Errors in Your Speaking and Writing*. New York: Collier/Macmillian, 1987.

A Manual of Style, 13th Edition. Chicago: The University of Chicago Press, 1982. A standard working resource of editors, authors, advertisers, typographers, proofreaders, and printers since 1906.

Mullins, Carolyn J. *The Complete Writing Guide to Preparing Reports, Proposals, Memos, Etc.* Englewood Cliffs, NJ: Spectrum/Prentice Hall, 1980.

Munter, Mary. *Guide to Managerial Comunication*, 2nd ed. Englewood Cliffs, NJ: Prentice Hall, Inc., 1982.

Nelson, Robert B. *The Job Hunt: The Biggest Job You'll Ever Have.* Berkeley: Ten Speed Press, 1986.

Jordan, Lewis. *The New York Times Manual of Style and Usage.* New York: Times Books, 1976. An enlarged edition of guidelines for those who write and edit. Easy to use and very complete.

Parker, Yana. *The Damn Good Resume Guide.* Berkeley: Ten Speed Press, 1983. New ideas and formats on functional resume writing.

Plotnik, Arthur. *The Elements of Editing: A Modern Guide for Editors and Journalists.* New York: Collier/Macmillian, 1982.

Robertson, Mary and Perkins, W. E. *Effective Correspondence for Colleges*, 5th ed. Palo Alto: South-Western Publishing, 1983.

Roddick, Ellen. *Writing That Means Business: How to Get Your Message Across Simply and Effectively.* New York: Collier/Macmillian, 1984.

Sabin, William. *The Gregg Reference Manual*, 6th Edition. New York: McGraw-Hill, 1985.

Strunk, William, Jr., and White, E. B. *The Elements of Style.* New York: Macmillan, 1959. Probably the best and briefest statement of the principal requirements for plain English.

Temple, Michael. *A Pocket Guide to Correct English.* New York: Barron's, 1978.

Style Manual. Washington, D.C.: U.S. Government Printing Office, 1984.

Warren, Thomas L. *Technical Communication.* Totowa, NJ: Littlefield, Adams and Co., 1978.

Warringer, John E., Whitten, Mary E., and Griffith, Francis. *English Grammar and Composition.* New York: Harcourt Brace Jovanovich, 1977. Extensive grammatical explanations, rules of composition and practice exercises to improve writing.

Webster's New World Misspeller's Dictionary. New York: Simon and Schuster, 1983. Over 15,000 common misspellings and their correct spellings. A unique and valuable reference guide.

Westheimer, Patricia H. *The Perfect Memo.* Glenview, IL: Scott, Foresman and Co., 1988.

Westheimer, Patricia H. *Power Writing for Executive Women.* Glenview, IL: Scott, Foresman and Co., 1989.

Westheimer, Patricia H., and Gibbs, Vicki T. *How to Write Like an Executive.* Glenview, IL: Scott, Foresman and Co., 1989.

Westheimer, Patricia H., and Senteney, Jacqueline S. *The Executive Style Book.* Glenview, IL: Scott, Foresman and Co., 1988.

INDEX